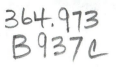

THE CRIMINAL JUSTICE SYSTEM

RONALD G. BURNS

Texas Christian University

PEARSON

Prentice
Hall

Upper Saddle River, New Jersey 07458

Library of Congress Cataloging-in-Publication Data

Burns, Ronald G.,
 The criminal justice system / Ronald G. Burns.
   p. cm.
 Includes bibliographical references and index.
 ISBN 0-13-170507-5 (alk. paper)
 1. Criminal justice, Administration of—United States. I. Title.
HV9950.B87 2006
364.973—dc22

2005023203

Executive Editor: Frank Mortimer, Jr.
Assistant Editor: Mayda Bosco
Marketing Manager: Adam Kloza
Editorial Assistant: Kelly Krug
Production Editor: Mike Remillard, Pine Tree Composition, Inc.
Production Liaison: Barbara Marttine Cappuccio
Director of Manufacturing and Production: Bruce Johnson
Managing Editor: Mary Carnis
Manufacturing Manager: Ilene Sanford
Manufacturing Buyer: Cathleen Petersen
Senior Design Coordinator: Mary Siener
Cover Design: Viki Kane
Formatting and Interior Design: Pine Tree Composition, Inc.
Printing and Binding: Banta Harrisonburg

Pearson Education LTD.
Pearson Education Singapore, Pte. Ltd
Pearson Education, Canada, Ltd
Pearson Education—Japan
Pearson Education Australia PTY, Limited
Pearson Education North Asia Ltd
Pearson Educación de Mexico, S.A. de C.V.
Pearson Education Malaysia, Pte. Ltd

10 9 8 7 6 5 4 3 2
ISBN 0-13-1705075

For Lisa, Ryan, Lily, and Maggie

CONTENTS

PREFACE

Most people have some understanding of how our system of justice works. Unfortunately, many integral parts of the system are absent from our perceptions of criminal case processing. The Criminal Justice System is designed to address this concern by simplifying criminal case processing through clearly identifying how one enters and is processed through the entire system. It is important for us to clearly understand how things work within our justice systems simply because of the increasingly integral roles crime and justice assume in everyday society. The pages that follow simplify the steps of the criminal justice system by describing the most common sequence of events in criminal case processing.

The idea for this work emerged from years of teaching Introduction to Criminal Justice to undergraduates. In structuring my introductory criminal justice course, I follow the format of the very impressive cadre of available introductory criminal justice texts. Section I provides a foundation for the course, covering issues regarding law, criminology, the extent and nature of crime, and so on; Section II covers various aspects in policing; and the third and fourth sections cover courts and corrections, respectively. The available introductory criminal justice texts do a superb job introducing readers to all aspects of criminal justice. This book focuses specifically on the steps involved in criminal case processing; it provides a concise description of the functioning of the criminal justice system.

The book is organized according to the steps of the criminal justice system, and the components of the system involved with those steps. The first section, "Entry into the System," examines the preliminary phases of criminal case processing. The chapters in this section address crime reporting practices, the investigation of criminal behavior, arrest practices, and booking and charging practices. The second section covers court-related practices prior to trial, including the initial appearance, preliminary and grand jury hearings, and arraignments. The third section addresses trials, sentencing, and appeals. The fourth and final section, "Corrections," includes chapters on probation, intermediate sanctions, incarceration and capital punishment, and release and reentry. With the exception of the final section, the chapters are presented in the sequential order that they exist in the criminal justice system.

In an attempt to make the material "come to life," the discussion of case processing is supplemented by a fictitious account of an offender, James Bower, who proceeds through the system. Each chapter includes a brief account of how James was processed and what he experienced. Each chapter also includes a "Point–Counterpoint" section in which a critical issue is addressed from different viewpoints. Short essay questions and critical thinking exercises accompany each chapter, as does a list of suggested readings.

The functioning and interrelatedness of police, courts, and corrections constitute what is considered "the criminal justice system," but is it really a system? Several question the appropriateness of referring to a particular criminal justice system, or referring to our practices of dispensing justice as a "system" (e.g., Adler, Mueller, & Laufer, 2003). The idea of a system conjures images of a smooth, working operation that offers appropriate actions and reactions concerning the common and problematic issues that arise. Does our system fit this description? Strong arguments could be made that our system is, or is not, truly a system.

Additional concerns arise when one considers the true meaning of the term *justice,* which means many different things to different people. *Justice* is often defined using terms such as *fairness* and *equity,* terms whose definitions remain subject to interpretation. Eskridge (1999, p. 11) suggests the presence of four elements is required to dispense absolute justice: (1) the absolute ability to identify law violators; (2) the absolute ability to apprehend law violators; (3) the absolute ability to punish law violators; and (4) the absolute ability to identify the intent of law violators. Our current systems of justice simply do not have the resources nor the ability to bring about these four elements. In turn, we make great efforts to approach justice, yet reaching justice is not always possible and we are forced to find some agreement regarding what is just. Determining what constitutes justice is not easily done, as the term means different things to various individuals and groups. For instance, liberals may view justice as rehabilitating offenders. Conservatives may view justice as incarcerating criminals. Bringing these and other groups into agreement as to what constitutes justice further clouds our understanding of what, specifically, constitutes a criminal justice system.

Adding confusion is the common perception that there is a single criminal justice system. Similar to the term *crime,* which signifies a variety of behaviors and has several meanings, the term *criminal justice system* is also nondescript in that there is no one system per se. Each state and the federal government has a criminal justice system, and criminal justice is also administered at the county and local levels. Our decentralized system of criminal justice dictates that jurisdictions other than the federal government provide protection and service for citizens. Criminal justice in the United States is composed of various individual systems, although the systems are tied together and grounded in the due process guarantees identified within the U.S. Constitution.

The bulk of the present book focuses on criminal justice at the state and local levels simply because most criminal case processing occurs at these levels. The federal system of criminal justice processes federal crimes, which constitute a minority of criminal cases processed in the United States. Differences between state/local and federal criminal case processing are noted in places, however, emphasis is placed on state/local-level criminal case processing.

For the purposes of this work, the term *criminal justice system* refers to the collective body of criminal justice systems within the United States. One must keep in mind that, because there are so many individual systems of justice, there are differences among jurisdictions. What follows is a discussion of general practices within these systems. Variations in practices among jurisdictions are noted in places.

Sir Arthur Conan Doyle, author of the Sherlock Holmes fiction books, wrote, "Crime is common. Logic is rare. Therefore it is upon the logic rather than upon the crime that you should dwell." While Doyle was referring to solving crime, his quote could also apply to addressing crime in general and our responses to illegal behavior. With the present work it is hoped that we can continue moving forward as we address crime and justice. It is hoped that readers will better understand the criminal justice system and continuously and emphatically incorporate logic in their approaches to crime and justice.

A special thanks is offered to all who contributed to this work, including friends, family, colleagues, the following reviewers: Professor Joseph Davey, Rowan University, Glassboro, NJ; Professor Edwin Ueckert, Blinn College, Brenham, TX; Professor Alison McKenney Brown, Wichita State University, Wichita, Kansas; and everyone at Prentice Hall, especially Frank Mortimer and Mayda Bosco. Your input and efforts are truly appreciated.

Ronald Burns
Texas Christian University

ENTRY INTO THE SYSTEM

1 REPORTED AND OBSERVED CRIME

A young woman, Jane Dahlman, was returning to her car from an evening of dinner and a movie with friends when she was accosted on a dark, semi-deserted street by a young male (James Bower). The man threatened her with a .38 caliber gun and demanded her purse and jewelry. The woman complied and the offender ran off without physically harming the victim. Realizing that her cell phone and keys were in her purse, the frightened woman contemplated her next move. She returned to the movie theater and found none of her friends. She approached the ticket window and asked for a phone to call the police. The theater cashier phoned the police who arrived shortly thereafter. The police asked for a description of the offender, whom the woman could only describe as a white male in his mid-twenties. The police asked Jane if she suffered any physical injuries (she had not), and then took her contact information and informed her that they would soon be in touch. In the meantime, the woman was forced to spend the night at a friend's house and begin the process of contacting a locksmith, canceling her credit card and cell phone accounts, and addressing the many other inconveniences associated with this type of victimization.

The situation described above involves one form of crime and victimization. The victim in this case was clearly robbed, and reported the crime to the police. Her report will contribute to the crime rate, and initiate law enforcement efforts to apprehend the offender. Assuming a successful apprehension, the suspect will be processed and turned over to the courts where he will face adjudication. Assuming he pleads or is found guilty, he will then face some penalty. The lives of the offender and victim will change as a result of this particular incident. Jane will face many inconveniences putting her life back together (e.g., changing locks, canceling phone and credit card accounts, and overcoming the fear of a violent victimization), while James will evade the law and if apprehended will become part of the criminal justice system. This case will be followed throughout each chapter of this book, with the goal of helping readers better understand how the system works. The reader will hopefully become more familiar with the workings of the criminal justice system through closely following this particular case.

Crime is a complex and variable term that can be simply defined as "An act committed or omitted in violation of a law forbidding or commanding it, for which the possible penalties upon conviction for an adult include incarceration . . ." (Rush, 2003, p. 91). The term *crime* lacks some clarity, considering that many different behaviors can be recognized as being in violation of a law. For instance, the illegal gambler is a criminal much the same as the murderer. While distinctions are made between types of crime (e.g., property and violent, felony and misdemeanor), the commonality among all crimes is that they involve violations of a law. Absent from this brief description of crime are those violations that may be harmful, although not (yet?) recognized by criminal law.

Among the more pressing questions surrounding crime are who commits crime and why? While these and other questions continuously challenge researchers, bits of evidence emerge from the extensive and growing body of criminological research. Despite disagreements regarding the specific causes of crime, there is consensus that multiple factors contribute to illegal behavior. No single factor causes crime. Similarly, no one particular type of person commits crime as, for example, criminals can be wealthy or poor, minority or nonminority, male or female.

MEASURED, OBSERVED, AND REPORTED CRIME

We often hear media reports suggesting that "crime has gone down (or up) this year," with the report followed by statistics highlighting the increase or decrease and brief explanations for the change. The reports often identify the source of the data, yet rarely delve into the limitations of the data collection instrument. While the quality of crime data in the United States has evolved over the years, it remains that crime is very difficult to measure. The three primary approaches used to measure crime include official government statistics on criminal behavior (e.g., the Uniform Crime Report [UCR] and National Incident-Based Reporting System [NIBRS]), and victimization (e.g., the National Crime Victimization Survey [NCVS]), and self-report studies. From these reports we get different views of the nature and extent of crime in our society. Each approach has limitations that are well documented (e.g., Kappeler & Potter, 2005; Shelden & Brown, 2003), which in turn obscure our ability to clearly identify the true nature and extent of crime. One particular limitation inherent in each measurement is their failure to capture information on all crimes, primarily since there is a vast difference between the number of crimes committed and reported.

To demonstrate the limitations of our primary sources of data collection, consider how each method relies on crime reporting. With the exception of prison statistics, the UCR is the "oldest extant national crime data system in the United States" (Rosen, 1995, p. 215). Introduced in 1930, it is argued that the UCR was created by the International Association of Chiefs of Police in an attempt to counter what was recognized as a disparaging view of crime (and the police) offered by the press (Rosen, 1995). While many improvements were made to the UCR, several limitations remain, particularly with regard to crime reporting practices. For instance, the UCR is a measure of crimes reported to the police, not the actual number of crimes committed. Unfortunately, a substantial portion of crime goes unreported. The recently introduced NIBRS, which provides greater detail of criminal events, should reduce many of the existing limitations of the UCR, although it too is far from perfect.

The NCVS was created with the intent to better understand criminal victimization. It is recognized for its attempts to measure the dark figure of crime, or those crimes that are not reported to police. While the NCVS undoubtedly adds to our understanding of crime and victimization, its limitations include subject underreporting. Why are crimes underreported in the NCVS? There are many answers to this question, including the sensitivity of crime in general (e.g., some may not wish to disclose what could be seen as discomforting information); practices of rationalizing, normalizing, or neutralizing victimization (e.g., "It's not crime, I deserved it"); and the inaccessibility of particular groups of people (e.g., runaways, the homeless). These factors contributing to the underreporting of crime are also limitations of many self-report surveys.

WHO REPORTS CRIME?

Most crime is brought to the attention of police via citizen reports. Crime is also reported by informants, offenders who confess to their actions, and the police, particularly through patrol practices and undercover operations.

Answering the question, "Who reports crime?" requires consideration of the vagueness of the term *crime*. For instance, it would seem as if gender would not affect the likelihood of reporting a stolen car. However, would gender affect the likelihood of reporting domestic abuse? Reports of rape or sexual assault? Research in this area is far from conclusive, although it is widely agreed that crime reporting practices vary by type of crime and individuals. Understanding why only some people report crime involves consideration of a variety of factors, perhaps the most important being the seriousness of the crime and the relationship between victim and offender.

Police must primarily rely on citizen reports of crime simply because they personally encounter only about 4–5% of all crimes (Reiss, 1971; Walker & Katz, 2002). Hart and Rennison (2003) noted that only 39% of the roughly 25.4 million violent and property crimes committed against individuals age 12 or older were reported to the police. Observed together these figures suggest that a substantial portion of crime is not brought to the attention of the police.

The nonreporting of crime has been examined by researchers and what we currently know sheds light on areas of needed improvement in the criminal justice system, particularly with regard to victim's services. In general, there is no single reason why victims do not report crime. For instance, in her analyses of National Crime Survey data, Harlow (1985) found that the type of crime, the victim's gender and race, the value of the theft or property damage, and the extent to which the victim was threatened or injured were among the variables associated with reporting rates.

In summarizing the literature on crime reporting, Bennett and Wiegand (1994) offer three areas of correlates that help explain crime reporting practices: incident (or crime)-specific factors, individual-specific factors, and environment-specific factors. Incident-specific correlates appear to offer the most explanatory power with regard to crime reporting practices (Bennett & Wiegand, 1994), although a variety of factors from each area explain why only some choose to report crime.

Incident-Specific Factors

Some researchers suggest incident-specific factors are the most important determinants of the decision by victims to report crime. Research suggests that minor property offenses constitute a great deal of the pool of unreported crimes (e.g., Skogan, 1977), as the likelihood of someone reporting a crime largely depends on the seriousness of the offense (e.g., Skogan, 1976). Other incident-specific factors such as fear of reprisal may influence victim reporting. Skogan (1977) noted that interpersonal crimes that go unreported are less likely to involve injury, involve small financial losses, and are less likely to involve weapons.

Fear of reprisal, or retaliation for reporting a crime, influences some reporting practices. Some crimes (particularly violent crime) are not reported out of a victim's fear of reprisal (e.g., Elias, 1986). The reporting of domestic violence incidents is sometimes influenced by the victim's economic dependence on the offender (e.g., Pagelow, 1984) and fear of reprisal. For instance, it is well established that domestic violence incidents are less likely to be reported to the police than violence between strangers (Block, 1974). Kidd and Chayet (1984) argue that the nonreporting of crime is the result of a combination of factors acting together, or alone, including victim fear of reprisal, victim fear in general, victim feelings of helplessness, and a lack of support from the police.

Recent figures suggest the most common (20%) reason why victims did not report violent crime was their belief that the incident was a private or personal matter. Fear of reprisal constituted only 5% of the reasons why victims did not report a violent crime (Hart & Rennison, 2003). The same report noted that the most common reasons for reporting violent crime were to prevent future violence and to stop the offender.

Individual-Specific Factors

Individual characteristics of victims appear to play a less significant role in crime reporting practices than do incident-specific factors (e.g., Bennett & Wiegand, 1994), although some findings suggest that several characteristics do influence crime reporting practices. For example, some research suggests that the young (e.g., Skogan, 1976) or those under age 35 (e.g., Hindelang & Gottfredson, 1976) are less likely to report victimization than other groups, and income appears to have a slight positive relationship with crime reporting (e.g., Hindelang & Gottfredson, 1976). Skogan (1976) noted that the small group of individuals in the extremely high income group are more likely to report property offenses yet less likely to report violent victimizations. Women appear to report violent victimizations more than men (e.g., Hart & Rennison, 2003); however, it does not appear that race influences victimization reporting practices (e.g., Walker & Katz, 2002).

Perhaps the strongest individual-level predictors of victimization reporting involve a victim's experiences with, perceptions of, and attitudes toward the police. For instance, Skogan (1976) found that victims appear to respond to their own beliefs that some type of action will result from their reporting victimization. Others note that a negative attitude toward the police may result in victims being less likely to report an incident (e.g., Shapland, Willmore, & Duff, 1985). Some suggest that positive prior experiences with the police results in a greater likelihood of victims cooperating with authorities (e.g., Conaway & Lohr, 1994), and it was noted that victims are less likely to report crimes due to their wish to avoid further victimization; the costs associated with contacting the police (e.g., costs measured in time); and the feelings of helplessness sometimes associated with being victimized (e.g., Kidd & Chayet, 1984).

Environment-Specific Factors

Neighborhood characteristics appear to influence victim reporting practices (e.g., Ruback, Greenberg, & Westcott, 1984), although it is argued that environment or community factors appear to play the most limited role in crime reporting (e.g., Bennett & Wiegand, 1994). For instance, Gottfredson and Hindelang (1979) found that, controlling for seriousness of crime, community factors are only minimally associated with crime reporting.

It does appear, however, that the poor, the group most often victimized, are less likely to report crime than those in other socioeconomic categories. Black (1983) suggests that the poor are less likely to seek formal intervention if they are less supportive of official means of social control. It appears that low-income communities are more resistant than other groups toward formal intervention, as informal interventions seem to be preferable in handling particular forms of grievances. The relationship between environment-specific factors and crime reporting is summarized by Bennett and Wiegand who note: "that seriousness of crime is the key to reporting and that individuals and neighborhood correlates possibly operate to enhance, mitigate, or control the influence of crime seriousness" (1994, p. 137).

Having identified factors related to crime reporting, we must ask the questions: How and why should victims report crime? Crime comes to the attention of law enforcement via three avenues: (1) citizen reports, (2) law enforcement personnel observing criminal behavior, and (3) proactive police investigations (Walker & Katz, 2002). Police learn of crime most often through citizen reports; however, most victims do not report crimes. Citizens often report crimes via an emergency telephone number designated to provide rapid police response, such as 911. The likelihood of an arrest being made is greatly increased when police are summoned while the crime is in progress or immediately thereafter. In other words, a crucial factor influencing the likelihood of an arrest is the quickness with which the victim calls the police (Spelman & Brown, 1984). Spelman and Brown (1984) note that delays by both victims and witnesses in contacting the police following victimization (and thus limiting the likelihood that an arrest will be made) include individuals finding the situation ambiguous (e.g., "Was it a crime?"), the initiation of coping strategies (e.g., offering assistance to the victim), and seeking advice prior to contacting the police. The availability of a telephone is another crucial factor in immediately contacting the police, although the increased use of cell phones encourages crime reporting. The more technologically advanced phones, which enable victims or witnesses to conveniently take a photograph, facilitate the apprehension and conviction of criminals.

The commission of a crime does not automatically activate a response from the criminal justice system. In other words, the police cannot be expected to solve crimes not brought to their attention. Thus, there are many reasons why victims *should* report crime, particularly since 95% of all crimes known to police are brought to their attention by crime reporting (Reiss, 1971). The most significant consequences of not reporting crime include: (1) the negative impact on the deterrent capability of the criminal justice system; (2) the encouragement of misguided police resources; (3) the limited effectiveness of victim benefits and services; and (4) increased insurance costs (Skogan, 1977). Of particular importance with regard to nonreporting is the possibility of continued criminal behavior on behalf of the offender whose actions went unreported, which in turn could impact citizen fear. In sum, we can be certain that reporting crime is a substantial first step in criminal case processing.

WRAP-UP

Sparks, Genn, and Dodd (1977) identify the progression of events beginning with crime commission through what is recognized as "crime known to police." The process begins with individuals perceiving that a particular act occurred (using the case study provided at the beginning of the chapter, Jane would recognize that she was attacked). The act must then be recognized as outside the boundaries of the law (e.g., Jane would recognize the attack as criminal), and then reported to the police who redefine the event (e.g., the police would determine that Jane was robbed). The recording process follows, as actions are compiled into recognizable categories. Bear in mind that at any one of these steps the victim may decline or hesitate to report crime, or that the actual criminal event may become recoded through various filtering processes (e.g., the police, the victim, witnesses).

This chapter opened with an account of Jane Dahlman's victimization, and addressed the observation and reporting of crime. Based on existing research regarding who reports crime and why, it was expected that Jane would report her victimization, primarily because robbery is a serious crime. Jane would have been less likely to contact the police had her victimization simply involved someone stealing CDs from her open convertible while she was out with friends. Now that we have a better understanding of the nature of crime, and how and why it is reported, it is time to closely examine the workings of the criminal justice system. The following chapters specifically address criminal case processing in sequential order. The step following the commission and reporting of a crime is police investigation of the incident.

Point–Counterpoint

It is suggested that police practices disproportionately impact minority groups, for instance, through heavily allocating patrol resources in minority neighborhoods. Others suggest patrol is disproportionately located in these areas because a great deal of crime occurs in these neighborhoods. *Do current practices of identifying crime disproportionately affect minority groups?*

Yes: It is true that one's race/ethnicity alone does not impact one's likelihood of reporting crime to the police, much like one's race/ethnicity alone does not affect one's likelihood to commit crime. However, social factors can and do impact minority reporting of crime. It is well established that minorities have, historically, had an unsavory relationship with the police. Research strongly suggests that one's relationship or prior experience with the police impacts their decision to report crime. As such, minorities would be less likely than nonminorities to contact the police. Similarly, police patrol is disproportionately located in minority neighborhoods. Even though police observe only a small fraction of crime, their disproportionate presence in minority neighborhoods does result in greater recognition of crimes committed by minorities; a small percentage of a large number of crimes is still of concern.

No: It is argued that there are limited or no differences in the crime reporting practices of minorities and nonminorities. Research suggests that race does not play a role in determining who reports crime. For instance, in the 1970s Skogan (1976, 1977) found that race does not appear to influence crime reporting. Some would argue that current practices of iden-

tifying crime disproportionately affects minority groups because police disproportionately patrol these areas and are more likely to identify offenses simply by their mere presence in the area. This argument is tempered by the fact that the overwhelming majority of crime is brought to the attention of police by citizen reports, not police observation.

Note: Keep in mind that the "Point–Counterpoint" arguments provided at the end of each chapter do not necessarily reflect the views of the author. The arguments provided in these sections are reflective of the literature surrounding the topics.

SUGGESTED READING

Bennett, R. R., & Wiegand, R. B. (1994). Observations on crime reporting in a developing nation. *Criminology, 32*(1), pp. 135–148.

Conaway, M. R., & Lohr, S. L. (1994). A longitudinal analysis of factors associated with reporting violent crimes to the police. *Journal of Quantitative Criminology, 10*(1), pp. 23–39.

Hart, T. C., & Rennison, C. (2003, March). *Reporting crime to the police, 1992–2000* (NCJ 195710). Washington, DC: Bureau of Justice Statistics.

Skogan, W. (1977). Dimensions on the dark figure of unreported crime. *Crime & Delinquency, 23*, pp. 41–50.

Spelman, W. G., & Brown, D. K. (1984). *Calling the police: Citizen reporting of serious crime.* Washington, DC: Police Executive Research Forum.

CRITICAL THINKING EXERCISES

1. Create a public service advertisement designed to encourage victims to report all forms of crime. Where would you place this advertisement? Who would you target?

2. Based on the research concerning crime reporting, rank-order the five types of crime you believe are most often reported.

3. Create a one-page survey designed to better understand who reports crime and why. What questions will you ask?

SHORT ESSAY QUESTIONS

1. Discuss how the UCR is dependent on the reporting of crime for accuracy.

2. What are the three areas of correlates that help explain crime reporting practices?

3. Identify and discuss the factors that appear to be strongly related to crime reporting.

4. Aside from victim complaints to police, how is crime brought to the attention of police?

5. Identify and discuss the case processing steps that occur beginning with crime commission and progressing through what is recognized as "crime known to police."

2 INVESTIGATION

Jane's victimization following a night out with her friends prompted immediate police response since it was a violent crime and the third robbery in the neighborhood during the past month. After gathering information about the attack from Jane, the police began a preliminary investigation in which they searched the area surrounding the incident for clues. In the area, they found a cigarette lighter, which they carefully placed in a protective case to later inspect for fingerprints. During the follow-up investigation, the police knocked on doors of the apartments in the surrounding area asking tenants if they saw or heard anything related to the incident. A young man living in one of the apartments claimed to have seen a white male in his mid-twenties dressed in dark clothes running from a young woman around the time of the attack. The witness, Cedric Alexander, hadn't seen what transpired prior to the man running away and thought nothing of the situation. He didn't contact the police as he thought it was a non-criminal, private matter. The police asked Cedric if he would come to the police station to see if he could identify the perpetrator from a series of photographs. Cedric identified three suspects from the photo lineup. Police were then able to match the fingerprints on the lighter with one of the suspects, James Bower.

Along with patrol, investigation is one of the "most important units in a police department" (Cole & Smith, 2004, p. 198). It is the topic of many police dramas shown on television and in the movies (e.g., *CSI, NYPD Blue, Lethal Weapon*), with detectives depicted as law-and-order types whose lives are consumed with "catching the bad guy." Much of the general public's knowledge regarding detective work comes from the media, just as much of the public's understanding of crime is media-based. The romantic history of detective work in the likes of Sherlock Holmes, Dirty Harry, and Joe Friday have largely shaped the heroic, crime-fighting image of the detective (see Kuykendall, 1986, for a thorough account of the historical development of the municipal detective).

Crime investigation follows a report to the police. The nature of the investigation varies in many ways. For instance, it can be brief or extensive, it can be done by detectives or patrol officers, and it can be reactive or proactive. The nature of the crime and available resources often dictate the extent to which a crime is thoroughly investigated. For instance, a bicycle theft will not receive the same attention as a murder. Similarly, a crime involving one bicycle theft will not receive the level of attention of a crime involving the theft of seven bicycles. The nature of the offense also dictates who investigates, as, for instance, traffic offenses will likely be investigated by patrol officers, whereas sexual assaults will likely be investigated by detectives. Brandl (1993) found that the value of the stolen property and the likelihood of arrest affected how much effort police devoted to burglary and robbery cases, while Bayley (1994) suggested that the credible identification of a perpetrator and the seriousness of an offense impact a detective's decision to investigate a case.

Jane Dahlman's case likely prompted immediate police response due to the seriousness of the offense and because it was the third robbery in the area within the past month. Unfortunately, not all crimes receive such attention, as many police departments simply do not have the resources to investigate all crimes brought to their attention.

DECIDING TO INVESTIGATE

There is no concrete method of investigating crime, and the structure and organization of investigative units within police departments vary. Part of the excitement officers and detectives recognize in investigating crime is the variety and challenges posed by the uniqueness of each case. Investigators have reliable methods and tactics they use to investigate crime, and of course they must be cognizant of procedural law (laws that govern how the law is applied) during their investigation.

In many jurisdictions and certainly within large cities, police departments do not have the resources to thoroughly investigate every crime. In turn, they often prioritize and allocate investigative resources based on offense seriousness. What makes a crime serious? While each department, and officer/detective, may have their own beliefs regarding what constitutes a serious crime, several factors appear to consistently influence perceptions of crime. Among those factors are interpersonal harm, the loss incurred, and publicity surrounding the incident. For instance, violent crimes are recognized as more serious than property crimes, stolen automobiles receive more attention than stolen skateboards, and unsolved crimes repeatedly covered by the media will likely receive greater attention than those not brought to the public's attention.

Detectives also consider whether their investigative efforts will result in enough evidence to bring charges. Are there witnesses? Is there a suspect? Researchers found that victims in higher socioeconomic levels received greater investigative attention than those in lower levels (e.g., Waegel, 1981); however, it appears that the level of accessible evidence is the strongest predictor of the investigators' effort (e.g., Brandl, 1993). Given the need to prioritize cases, investigators may choose to forego investigating particular crimes, for instance, when there is not enough evidence.

WHO INVESTIGATES CRIME?

Researchers found that about 93% of local police departments investigated at least some type of crime during the 12-month period ending June 30, 2000, with roughly 58% of departments handling homicide investigations (Hickman & Reaves, 2003). Most large departments have specialized investigation divisions, for instance, a homicide division or an economic crime division. Other large departments, and most smaller departments, have investigators who are considered generalists and investigate all offenses. Patrol officers and detectives are assisted in their investigations by others, including technical experts such as forensic scientists and lab technicians, and other law enforcement agencies. On average, about 10–15% of a police department's sworn officers are located in a detective unit (Gaines, Kappeler, & Vaughn, 1999).

Detective work is generally more appealing to police than patrol work, primarily due to the higher level of prestige, the increased pay, the more flexible hours, and the reduced level of supervision. Not having to wear a uniform and the interesting nature of the work are also seen by some as advantages of detective work. Because their work involves little or no order maintenance or service work, investigators largely contribute to the image of police as crime fighters (Cole & Smith, 2004).

Investigating a crime is a reactionary process that sometimes involves proactive efforts, such as the use of sting and decoy operations. Upon responding to an observed or a reported crime, the police conduct a preliminary investigation. They interview victims, suspects, and witnesses. Information gathered from this stage is used to conduct a more elaborate investigation, should one be necessary. Bayley (1994) suggests that detectives, on the basis of the preliminary investigation, generally have a suspect in mind and attempt to build a case around this individual, as opposed to collecting the information with the intent to identify a suspect.

The general public is perhaps the most helpful group that investigates crime. The importance of citizen input is widely recognized as the most significant factor in solving crimes. Witnesses, victims, and other members of the public often have insightful information that can assist investigations. Current attempts to involve the general public in fighting crime focus on encouraging citizens to become more aware and thus more helpful with investigating crime. Chaiken, Greenwood, and Petersilia (1977, p. 216) noted earlier that "Police departments should initiate programs designed to enhance the victim's desire to cooperate fully with the police. Such programs might both increase apprehension rates and improve the quality of prosecutions." Recent proactive community policing efforts have significantly contributed to greater citizen participation.

WHAT'S INVOLVED IN A CRIMINAL INVESTIGATION?

An investigation typically begins with an officer responding to a reported crime. As noted in Chapter 1, how quickly the officer responds to the call largely influences the likelihood of arrest. Upon arriving on the scene, the officer is responsible for (1) safety procedures, which are the officer's first priority and include the well-being of officers and others at the crime scene and identifying and controlling dangerous individuals and/or situations; (2) emergency care, which includes giving aid to victim(s) and calling for medical attention; (3) securing the crime scene for investigation, which includes preserving evidence and controlling the movement of witnesses and onlookers; (4) turning over control of the scene to the investigator in charge; and (5) documenting the actions and observations to preserve as part of a permanent record (Wrobleski & Hess, 2003).

Proper documentation and thorough accountability of all evidence are necessary for a successful investigation, as evidenced in the O.J. Simpson case when the questionable series of events in preserving the infamous bloody glove and blood traces found in the suspect's car had some influence on the jury's decision to acquit. Of particular concern during an investigation is the collection and preservation of physical evidence, including fingerprints, blood, saliva, semen, skin, and weapons. Other forms of physical evidence, such as electronic information or documentation of economic transactions, can be more difficult to collect and analyze. Despite strong public belief that physical evidence is the most powerful determinant in solving crime, Bayley (1994) notes that physical evidence is not especially important in determining whether or not a case is investigated and it rarely leads to the identification of individuals not already suspected by the police. Physical evidence, however, is often used as confirmation or in support of existing evidence (Bayley, 1994).

The information collected during the preliminary investigation is forwarded to the appropriate investigating unit if the responding officer(s) fails to locate a suspect. These investigative units begin with a "cold" search, which entails, among other things, securing the crime scene; recording information pertaining to the crime; creating a visual depiction of the scene through sketching, photography, and measurements; obtaining, identifying, protecting, and storing evidence; interviewing and questioning suspects; and providing overall assistance in identifying suspects (Wrobleski & Hess, 2003, p. 204). Pressure to investigate newer, or "warmer," cases may dictate that the investigators shelve particular cases where few leads are available (Cole & Smith, 2004).

Many issues require attention in a criminal investigation. For instance, in preparing a case, an investigator must consider the victim's role in the crime. Although it is not always popular to recognize a victim as contributing to their victimization, thorough detective work involves consideration of all participants in the crime. Consider someone who intentionally burns their failing restaurant (an arsonist) for insurance purposes. The apparent victim in this case is the offender. Investigators must also consider the benefits of the crime. They ask: "Who benefited and who suffered?" Those benefiting will undoubtedly be considered during an investigation.

Investigators must also consider one's opportunity to commit a crime. For instance, James would not be considered a primary suspect in the robbery of Jane if he was at the stationhouse speaking with police officers at the time Jane was robbed. The same can be said for one's ability to commit crime. James would, again, not be considered a suspect if he was bedridden at the time of the offense. Finally, investigators should seek a *modus operandi,* or "a characteristic pattern of behavior repeated in a series of offenses that coincides with the pattern evidenced by a particular person or group of persons" (Rush, 2003, p. 229). Understanding the characteristics of a particular series of crimes could help locate the offender.

In identifying the significance of the information gathered at the preliminary investigation, Goldstein (1977) argues that investigators are generally faced with four options that dictate the approach they take. First, he argues that detectives should prepare the case for presentation to the prosecuting attorney following a crime in which the suspect is caught. Second, detectives should attempt to locate the suspect(s) in cases where he or she is identified but not apprehended. Third, detectives should identify which suspect(s) committed the crime in cases involving multiple suspects. Finally, detectives should start from scratch when there is no suspect.

INVESTIGATIVE TOOLS

The investigator's most effective tool may be their ability to communicate, simply because they're in the business of obtaining information from others. Aside from communication skills, other helpful tools and tactics investigators use include surveillance, police lineups, photo lineups, informants, decoys, sting operations, polygraph testing, and crime labs. Surveillance involves observing suspects to gain valuable information, and can be used in three manners: (1) *fixed surveillance* can be covert (e.g., through the use of undercover or plainclothes officers) or overt (through the use of uniformed officers); (2) *moving surveillance* requires unidentifiable vehicles to follow the target; and (3) *electronic surveillance* involves wiretaps and other electronic audiovisual tools, for instance, night viewing devices (Lyman, 1999).

Police lineups are used when there is an eyewitness who can potentially identify the suspect. Lineups typically use four to six individuals who line up against a wall. The witness is asked if they recognize the suspect. Although a lineup format is ingrained in modern-day police practices, lineups have been criticized on the grounds of suggestibility and a potential for prejudice (Weston & Lushbaugh, 2003). There is a move toward enhancing police lineups by showing witnesses the suspects individually instead of collectively, and making the lineups double-blind in the sense that the officer in charge and the witness are both unaware of who is the alleged culprit. The argument is that showing suspects individually decreases the likelihood of witnesses selecting the suspect who *most closely* resembles the offender, as opposed to selecting the suspect who *is* the offender. Adopting a double-blind approach arguably reduces the likelihood of officers subconsciously influencing witness selection (Kloberdanz, 2005). Photo lineups are used when a suspect is not in custody, for instance, in our case study of James Bower. In photo lineups investigators use photographs of the suspect and a minimum of five other individuals to see if the eyewitness can identify the suspect.

Informants can be extremely helpful with investigations of crime, although there is an identifiable risk involved in using them. "An informant is a human source of information in a criminal action whose identity must be protected" (Hess & Wrobleski, 2003, p. 53). Informants may be rewarded with money or a reduced sentence for their cooperation, although the idea of rewarding someone for doing what seems to be their civic duty is troubling to some. Credibility is also an issue with regard to using informants, as noted in a recent case involving detectives from the Dallas Police Department paying informants hundreds of thousands of dollars for what turned out to be incorrect information that led to bogus arrests.

Officers working in decoy units often place themselves in vulnerable positions hoping to attract criminals. The approach is based on the assumption that some level of criminality exists, and officers can better identify offenders through providing attractive targets. Decoys are similar to sting operations in which officers pose as criminals (e.g., as drug buyers or prostitutes) with the intent to gain access to offenders.

Polygraph testing measures an individual's physiological reactions to a serious of questions in an attempt to detect deception. Hess and Wrobleski (2003) note that polygraphs are used to clear suspects; locate evidence; or confirm victim, witness, and/or suspect statements. Polygraph results are rarely admissible in court (they're only used when stipulated by all parties), despite claims of 95% accuracy with regard to polygraph testing (Bennett & Hess, 2001). The U.S. Supreme Court ruled that there is no consensus that polygraph testing is reliable ("Supreme Court Finds," 1998).

Investigators are often assisted by the increasing number of crime analysis units found within large and small police departments (Wernicke & Stallo, 2000). Through the use of crime mapping, DNA analysis, and other methods of matching physical evidence to a crime scene and ultimately a suspect, crime labs are becoming increasingly important to investigators. Crime analysis units assist heavily in criminalistics, or the science of crime detection. Unfortunately, there is a significant backlog of cases waiting for crime lab analyses, particularly with regard to DNA analysis (e.g., "Report to the Attorney," 2003; Steadman, 2002), and budgeting issues are problematic in some departments.

WRAP-UP

Technology has undoubtedly changed the process and effectiveness of criminal investigations. For instance, computers have assisted investigations through enhanced fingerprint identification. Almost all large police departments use an automatic fingerprint identification system (AFIS) to electronically track and identify suspects based on their fingerprints. Some departments use biometrics, which measure physical characteristics such as voice. Furthermore, evidence can be tracked via a computerized evidence tracking system (ETS), which uses barcodes in attempts to better organize collected evidence. As of 2000, all police departments serving populations of at least 250,000 used computed-aided dispatch. Roughly 92% of these departments used in-field computers or terminals for assistance (Reaves & Hickman, 2002). Computers have also contributed to forensic science, as technology is being used to analyze fibers, DNA, and other forms of evidence that were once beyond the reach of detectives. The Internet provides investigators a wealth of information to investigate crimes, particularly with regard to investigative techniques, database sharing, and training opportunities.

It is presumed that greater integration of technology into detective work will increase the efficiency and effectiveness of investigations. Despite the increasingly prominent role technology plays in criminal investigations, citizen awareness remains one of, if not the most powerful, crime-fighting tools, as evidenced in the apprehension of James Bower.

Point–Counterpoint

Detective work is often glamorized in popular culture as the key to solving crime. Detective work is certainly responsible for solving some crimes; however, some question the ability of detective work to solve crime, arguing that such resources would be more effective if allocated elsewhere. *Is detective work necessary?*

Yes: Research identifies the limitations of detective work. Perhaps our expectations of detective work need to be reconsidered. We will undoubtedly be discouraged if we expect too much from follow-up investigations to solve crimes. However, detective work plays a significant role in fighting crime. The studies often used to demonstrate the limitations of detective work (e.g., Greenwood, Chaiken, and Petersilia, 1977; President's Commission on Law Enforcement and Administration of Justice, 1967) are dated. One must believe that with better crime-fighting technology and more professional police practices that detective work is much better today than it was 40–50 years ago. More recent research highlights the benefits of detective work. William and Snortum (1984) replicated the Greenwood and colleagues (1977) study and found similar results, although they noted that detective work provided valuable benefits through skilled interrogation and case-processing procedures. Eck (1984) found that preliminary and follow-up investigations were equally important in his study of burglary and robbery investigations. Wrobleski and Hess (2003, p. 196) noted that "The quality of investigative work can still affect the clearance rates of homicide, robbery, and commercial theft," adding that they should provide greater attention to the quality of the preliminary investigation.

No: Earlier research questioned the effectiveness of detective work in solving crimes. In their study of large police departments, Greenwood and colleagues (1977) found that identification of an offender by witnesses or suspects was the most significant factor in solving a crime. Walker (2001) notes that most crimes cleared by arrest are readily solved through having a solid lead at the beginning of the case, adding that information about the suspect is vital to solving crime. While detective work does have its benefits, as noted above, there are many limitations, leading some to question if we misappropriate resources by relying heavily on detectives to solve crimes. Instead of funding elaborate investigative units, perhaps we should use our resources to *prevent* crime. Detective work emphasizes the reactive nature of law enforcement.

SUGGESTED READING

Bayley, D. (1994). *Police for the future.* New York: Oxford University Press.

Bennett, W., & Hess, K. (2001). *Criminal investigation* (6th ed.). Belmont, CA: Wadsworth.

Brandl, S. (1993). The impact of case characteristics on detectives' decision making. *Justice Quarterly, 10*(3), pp. 395–416.

Chaiken, J., Greenwood, P., & Petersilia, J. (1977). The criminal investigation process: A summary report. *Policy Analysis, 3,* pp. 187–217.

Weston, P. B., & Lushbaugh, C. (2003). *Criminal investigation: Basic perspectives* (9th ed.). Upper Saddle River, NJ: Prentice Hall.

CRITICAL THINKING EXERCISES

1. Assume you are a detective with limited resources. Prioritize the Index crimes according to the amount of resources you believe should be allocated toward the investigation of each. Identify the percentage of resources you would direct toward each of the crimes.

2. How can we reorganize the role of criminal investigators to make them more effective? Design an investigative unit for a large city. Give due consideration to methods of improving current investigative practices.

3. Discuss what you perceive to be the media's influence on public perceptions and expectations of detective work. Have the media shaped our beliefs of the capabilities of criminal investigations? Should police departments and the public have lower expectations of investigative units?

SHORT ESSAY QUESTIONS

1. What factors influence the likelihood of detectives investigating and solving a crime?

2. What are the responsibilities of the first police officer to arrive at a crime scene?

3. What "tools" assist criminal investigators? Discuss which approach/tactic you believe provides the greatest resource in criminal investigations.

4. What are the ethical issues involved with using informants and decoy units?

5. What groups are involved with the investigation of crime? Which group provides the most helpful information?

3 ARREST

James decided to keep a low profile following his attack on Jane. Unfortunately for him, he had a prior record of arrest and his file was available for the photo lineup, leading to a witness identifying him as the robber. Officers, under the authority of an arrest warrant based on witness identification and a match between the fingerprints on the lighter and the fingerprints found in James's criminal file, arrested James at his home. James did not resist arrest and complied with the officers' commands. Although James knew he was in trouble, he felt any evidence used to make an arrest would be circumstantial, as he did not see any witnesses at the time of the attack and was unaware that he left any physical evidence (the lighter) at the scene. James was informed of his rights as he was led to the backseat of a patrol car. Investigators would soon begin questioning James regarding the incident in question and the string of robberies in the area.

Police are granted particular powers for the purposes of social control, including the power to arrest, which may be the most obvious example of society sacrificing freedoms for the sake of social control. Officers must be wary of procedural law when making arrests, and they must consider the appropriateness of arrests in particular situations. The power to arrest notably affects public perceptions of policing. Officers acting under the law may be viewed as illegally, inappropriately, or unnecessarily restricting freedoms. Citizens also maintain the power to arrest, although citizen arrests rarely occur. The most common form of citizen arrest involves victims apprehending offenders.

The police maintain great authority in their power to remove or restrain one's freedom. One of the more volatile aspects of arrest situations involves the power differential between suspects and the police. We, as a society, give police officers special powers to arrest and expect them to use the powers as necessary. By nature, arrest situations typically involve individuals who are not beyond breaking the law (offenders), which can perpetuate hostility toward representatives of the law (officers) who are often the ones wielding the most power. This combination of ingredients sometimes leads to explosive police–citizen encounters, although it is well established that most police–citizen encounters involve very little violence.

With police powers to arrest comes the requirement to strictly abide by procedural laws as they pertain to arrest situations. For instance, officers must establish that there exists probable cause to make the arrest, and it is important for officers to detail the events surrounding the encounter and recognize any and all pieces of evidence. Failing to abide by procedural law during arrest situations may result in any evidence seized during the unlawful arrest being deemed inadmissible in court, and any conviction being overturned. Wrongful arrests can result in civil lawsuits filed against the arresting officer and the police department initiating or authorizing the arrest.

Arrest statistics do not provide an accurate picture of crime in America simply because most crimes go unsolved. Using various government crime data sources, Cole and Smith (2004) argue that on average, half of all serious crimes will not be reported to the police, and only 20 percent of those offenses will be solved. In total, only 100 arrests are made for every 1,000 serious crimes. One can speculate that the arrest rate for nonserious crimes is lower than the 10% rate for serious crimes, simply because victims/witnesses would be disinclined to report less serious offenses and police would allocate fewer resources to nonserious crimes than they would serious crimes. The likelihood of arrest is influenced by the nature of the crime, with a greater percentage of interpersonal crimes resulting in arrest than property crimes.

WHO GETS ARRESTED AND WHY

In 1999 about 43.8 million individuals age 16 or older, or roughly 21% of all persons of this age, had contact with the police. While most (52%) of these contacts occurred as the result of a traffic stop, about 3% of the contacts involved police questioning a crime suspect (Langan, Greenfeld, Smith, Durose, & Levin, 2001). The rates of police contact for black and Hispanic suspects were higher than the rate of contact for white suspects, while suspects between the ages of 16 and 24 had a higher rate of contact with the police than those in other age brackets (Langan et al., 2001).

Most arrests involve relatively minor offenses. For instance, Rainville and Reaves (2003) found that most arrests are made for Part II crimes, or what are generally considered less serious crimes than Part I offenses. Of the Part II crime arrests, most fall into the category "All other" and include crimes such as violations of local ordinances, probation and parole violations, and failing to appear in court. A notable percentage of arrests are also made for drug abuse violations, driving under the influence, and "nonaggravated assaults." Of the Part I, or Index crimes that the UCR provides as an index of crime in society and are generally considered the more serious offenses, a large majority of arrests involve larceny-theft.

Several notable findings emerge upon consideration of arrest statistics with regard to race, gender, age, and class. For instance, Shelden and Brown (2003) point out that African Americans constitute about 12% of the U.S. population, yet account for 28% of all arrests. Females are increasingly represented in the overall arrest rate, accounting for 26.4% of those arrested for Index crimes in 2000, compared to 21.4% in 1985. With the exception of arson, adults are and always have been the majority of those arrested and far more likely to be arrested for Index crimes than juveniles. With regard to class, it is well established that those in the lower socioeconomic classes are far more likely than those in the middle and upper classes to be arrested (e.g., Lynch, Michalowski, & Groves, 2000), despite recent publicity involving the arrests of several high-profile white-collar criminals. Chambliss (1984) cites the visibility of transgressions by lower-class persons as a factor influencing their overrepresentation in arrest statistics.

The clearance rate of local police departments has remained steady since the 1970s, hovering around 20%. Recent statistics suggest that 19.7% of offenses known to police were cleared by arrest in 2002, with violent crimes (44.5%) far more likely to result in arrest than property crimes (16.4%; Federal Bureau of Investigation, 2003). Some police departments use clearance rates as an evaluation indicator of performance. In other words, the effectiveness of some departments is measured by their likelihood to make an arrest following a crime brought to their attention. One limitation to this practice concerns the fact that suspects are not necessarily guilty simply because they've been arrested. We must remember that all suspects and arrestees in the American system of justice are innocent until proven guilty. An arrest signifies probable cause to believe the suspect committed the crime.

DEFINITION/LEGAL REQUIREMENTS OF ARREST

Procedural law requires that arrests be based on officers having *probable cause* to believe that an individual committed a crime. An arrest involves restricting one's right to move about freely. The actual point at which someone is formally under arrest may be difficult to identify (e.g., Lyman, 1999), although the point of arrest is easily determined in most cases; it is when the suspect is taken into custody and restraints (e.g., handcuffs) are applied. In our case study involving James's assault on Jane, the point of arrest was evident when James acquiesced to the officers' request for James to put out his hands for handcuffing and the officers told him he was under arrest. In the real world, the actual point of arrest is not as clear. For instance, the police may stop and question individuals suspected by the police to have information about a crime. These people are sometimes arrested and other times released, depending on the probable cause to arrest (Lyman, 1999). Specifically, a formal arrest occurs when three conditions exist: (1) police believe a crime has been, or will be, committed; (2) the arrestee is deprived of their freedom; and (3) the suspect recognizes that he or she is in custody of the police and is no longer permitted to voluntarily move about.

The laws of arrest vary by jurisdiction, although procedural law surrounding arrest warrants is largely consistent among departments. Warrants may be issued to initiate an arrest. An arrest warrant is issued by the court and provides the officer permission to formally arrest the individual named on the warrant. The warrant must be based on probable cause that the individual named in the warrant committed (or will commit) the unlawful act noted in the warrant.

"Under the strictest interpretation of the Constitution, a warrant should be required for all arrests" (Lyman, 1999, p. 205). However, most arrests are made without a warrant, as warrantless arrests are permissible only when the arresting officer has probable cause to believe the suspect committed, or will commit, a crime; and when the law permits the officer to do so. Most jurisdictions permit officers to make warrantless, felony arrests where probable cause exists, even though the officer may not have been present when the offense was committed. In the case of misdemeanors, probable cause and officer presence are required for warrantless arrests. Warrantless arrests generally require prompt probable cause hearings before a magistrate.

The 1966 case *Miranda* v. *Arizona* largely influenced police procedural law. In *Miranda,* the Supreme Court ruled that Ernesto Miranda's conviction was unconstitutional in that prior to police interrogation, suspects should be provided information pertaining to their Fifth Amendment rights against self-incrimination. As a result, law enforcement officials are required to inform suspects of their *Miranda* rights prior to questioning to ensure that suspect rights are protected and that proper warning is given to suspects at the time of their arrest. Most of us are familiar with the text of the *Miranda* warning, which informs suspects of their Fifth Amendment rights ("You have the right to remain silent. . . ."). It is widely believed that any arrest must begin with officers informing suspects of their protections from self-incrimination; however, the *Miranda* warning is not required unless the suspect is to be interrogated following arrest. Reading a suspect their *Miranda* rights prior to interrogation is but one piece of procedural law officers are required to obey when making an arrest (see Ferdico, 1996, for a thorough account of procedural law as it pertains to making an arrest).

ARREST AND DISCRETION

Police officers maintain a great deal of discretion in most aspects of their duties. Determining whether or not to make an arrest and how to conduct the arrest are two very important decisions officers make. It is well understood by those who study police discretion that selective enforcement of the law is the norm among officers. For instance, Black (1980) reported that police made arrests in only about half of all situations in which there was legal sufficiency to do so, suggesting that a great deal of consideration and decision making is involved in policing. Given the serious consequences associated with an arrest and the fact that arrests typically occur in low-visibility situations (e.g., compared to situations involving other criminal justice personnel, such as judges who preside in a courtroom), it seems police officers are provided powers not found in just about all other occupations. How and when they make arrests has been the topic of extensive observation and discussion.

Many of us have been pulled over while driving and were given either a citation or a warning. What influences some officers to issue citations while others, under similar conditions, will let traffic law violators go with a mere warning? Why do the police make arrests in only about half of all cases in which an arrest is justified? Answering these questions requires understanding police use of discretion, or understanding why the police behave as they do. To better understand officer behavior we must consider the factors contributing to the likelihood of police making an arrest. Much has been written about police use of discretion (e.g., Brooks, 2005; Sherman, 1980; Smith & Visher, 1981), with the bulk of this work suggesting that no particular factor directly influences police practices, although some factors are more strongly related to police practices than others. The factors identified as influencing police officer decisions to make an arrest are often categorized into situational factors, characteristics of the arresting officer and suspect, and environmental factors.

Situational Factors

Situational factors, which have received most of the research attention with regard to assessments of police–citizen interactions, pertain to characteristics of the interaction between suspects and police. Prominent among the situational variables related to officer decisions to arrest is the seriousness of the offense. For instance, in their study of street-level justice, Smith and Visher (1981, p. 173) found that "police decisions to invoke the law reflect the gravity of the offense."

Officer Characteristics

Officer characteristics include demographic variables and attitudinal characteristics, and offer some explanation of police discretion. For instance, Mastrofski, Worden, and Snipes (1995) found that officers who were more positive toward community policing were less likely to effect an arrest. Although officer characteristics offer some insight into officer arrest powers, these variables are not recognized as the most powerful predictors of police behavior (e.g., Riksheim & Chermak, 1993).

Suspect Characteristics

Suspect characteristics also contribute to our knowledge of police practices. For instance, researchers observed the relationship between police discretionary behavior and suspect race, gender, age, demeanor, socioeconomic status, and other variables. The literature surrounding police decisions to arrest and suspect characteristics is mixed. For example, some suggest that suspect race influences the likelihood of arrest, with black suspects more likely than whites to be arrested (e.g., Smith & Visher, 1981), whereas others found no evidence of officers treating minority suspects more punitively (e.g., Klinger, 1996)

Environmental Factors

Environmental, or neighborhood, factors include variables that extend beyond the immediate vicinity of an arrest. Neighborhood crime rates and socioeconomic levels are among the more common variables included in measurements of crime and justice. For instance, it is generally agreed that higher arrest rates occur in lower socioeconomic areas (e.g., Smith & Klein, 1984).

Officers are sometimes required to use physical force during an arrest, including the use of handcuffs/restraints, verbal commands, and weapons/tactics. The use of force could also involve nontraditional tactics such as vehicle rammings. Much like officer decision making in arrest situations, decisions to use force during arrest situations are based on several competing factors. Officers are generally required to use only the amount of force necessary to subdue the suspect. This rule sometimes requires split-second interpretation by officers regarding whether or not to use force, and what levels of force are appropriate. Research suggests that situational factors, such as the suspect's behavior, and whether or not they possess a weapon have the greatest impact on officer decisions to use force (e.g., Burns & Crawford, 2002).

WRAP-UP

To better understand police discretion in arrest situations, consider the factors surrounding James's arrest. The decision to arrest James was simple: an eyewitness account and matching fingerprints clearly provided probable cause. The situation dictated a low level of discretion with arrest the appropriate option. In cases such as this, the decision to arrest is easy. In other arrest situations a series of variables must be considered, sometimes in a matter of moments.

Arrest is the suspect's formal entry into the criminal justice system. It is the beginning of a series of steps that could ultimately result in the punishment of the suspect. The criminal justice system, however, is a filtering process in which offenders are removed from the system at various steps and for different reasons. A lack of evidence, for instance, may result in the arrest being dropped and the suspect freed. The possibility of a suspect being freed from the system applies to all stages of the criminal justice system.

Point–Counterpoint

One of the most recognizable individual rights is the protection from self-incrimination via the *Miranda* warning. However, some suggest it is no longer necessary to inform suspects of their rights. *Should we abolish the* Miranda *warning?*

Yes: Some suggest the *Miranda* warning is an artifact of the 1960s Warren Court when the Supreme Court supported legislation that provided too many protections for the accused. It is also believed that requiring officers to inform citizens of their rights provides an unnecessary burden on attempts to catch criminals. Aside from having to inform suspects of their rights, which may result in them refusing to answer questions, investigators are burdened by having to invest additional resources in seeking other types of evidence to establish probable cause. As a result, some crimes will go unsolved and citizens will be at greater risk of victimization because of either a technicality in which officers failed to inform a suspect of their rights or a confession could not be elicited following a suspect being told of their rights. Furthermore, citizens should be aware of their rights without having officers or investigators inform them, just as they should be aware of what is legal or illegal.

No: Aside from the obvious benefit of providing protection from self-incrimination, the *Miranda* warnings ensures that everyone, from the informed to the uninformed, is on a level playing field. The warning ensures that investigators don't unethically exploit one's ignorance of the law. The *Miranda* warning is also good for police–public relations, and contributes to community policing efforts. The warnings are symbolic in the sense that officers may be recognized by the public as concerned for individual rights. Perhaps most important, it is argued by both researchers and police that *Miranda*'s net impact on the confession rate is insignificant. Relatively few cases are dismissed due to a failure to issue a *Miranda* warning. Some officers note that *Miranda* warnings help them attain confessions they would otherwise have not been able to get.

SUGGESTED READING

Black, D. (1980). *Manners and customs of the police.* San Diego, CA: Academic Press.

Brooks, L. W. (2005). Police discretionary behavior: A study of style. In R. G. Dunham & G. P. Alpert (Eds.), *Critical issues in policing: Contemporary readings* (5th ed.; pp. 89–105). Prospect Heights, IL: Waveland.

Crawford, C., & Burns, R. (2002). Resisting arrest: Predictors of suspect non-compliance and use of force against police officers. *Police Practice and Research: An International Journal, 3*(2), pp. 105–117.

Sherman, L. (1980). Causes of police behavior: The current state of quantitative research. *Journal of Research in Crime and Delinquency, 17,* pp. 69–100.

Smith, D. A., & Klein, J. R. (1984). Police control of interpersonal disputes. *Social Problems, 31,* pp. 468–481.

CRITICAL THINKING EXERCISES

1. The research literature identifies several extralegal variables that influence officer decisions to arrest. What recruitment and selection tactics could be used to address the problems associated with biased policing, or officers disproportionately arresting particular groups?

2. Should local police departments be granted additional powers to arrest? Do you feel the specific restrictions placed on police officers (e.g., restrictions on search-and-seizure procedures, informing suspects of their Fifth Amendment rights) unduly hamper their ability to fight crime?

3. Design a one-page survey that could be administered to police officers to help us better understand the factors that influence officer decision making during an arrest. Consider the existing research in determining the variables you wish to measure in your study.

SHORT ESSAY QUESTIONS

1. When is an arrest warrant required?

2. What factors influence an officer's decision to make an arrest?

3. When is a suspect formally under arrest? Do you see any potential areas of misinterpretation with these requirements?

4. Should the police be required to read suspects their *Miranda* warnings? Is there anything that should be added to the warnings?

5. Who is arrested most often and why? What factors do you believe influence the likelihood of these groups being arrested most often?

4 BOOKING AND CHARGING

James was detained, booked, and interrogated at police headquarters. He was finger-printed and photographed, and a computer-based search was conducted to see if he was wanted for committing other crimes. James had no outstanding warrants, although the nature of his alleged attack led investigators to suspect he was responsible for the recent robberies in the area. James was taken to an interrogation room where detectives questioned him. James invoked his Fifth Amendment right to remain silent and did not respond to the detectives' questions. Having previously been through this process, James thought it was best to remain silent. James was placed in a station house holding cell following the interrogation. His initial appearance before a judge would occur the following morning. After reviewing the information pertaining to this case, the district attorney, in consultation with the arresting officer, decided to charge James with armed robbery.

BOOKING

Booking is the initial step in the disposition of arrestees. It involves creating an administrative record of the accused. In discussing the disposition of arrestees, Ferdico (1996, p. 144) notes, "The arrest of a person initiates a series of administrative and judicial processes dealing with the person and his or her property." Booking, sometimes referred to as "processing," typically involves a booking officer taking the suspect's personal information (e.g., name, date of birth, physical characteristics, etc.); recording information about the suspect's alleged offense; performing a background check on the suspect's criminal background; fingerprinting, photographing, and searching the suspect; confiscating any personal property maintained by the suspect, which will be returned upon release; and placing the suspect in a police station holding cell or a local jail, depending on jurisdictional practices. Booking is typically completed prior to the arrestee's initial appearance in court; however, it may occur after the initial appearance, or prior to and following the initial appearance (Ferdico, 1996).

Although booking procedures vary by jurisdiction and departments, booking officers are generally required to follow specific steps and be cognizant of several important considerations. The information gathered during booking can be categorized into four areas: (1) information based on searches of the suspect, (2) information pertaining to the suspect's possessions, (3) the suspect's personal data, and (4) information pertaining to the arrest. For instance, officers are required to perform a search of the suspect for the purposes of inmate safety (to reduce the risk of suicide or death in custody), the security of the facility, safeguarding prisoners' personal property, and for the safety of law enforcement officials. The search involves a shakedown of the offender, who should be instructed to empty their pockets and remove their coat, hat, shoes, belt, and so on. Except under emergency situations, male officers should search male suspects, and female officers search female suspects. Searches should be conducted out of view of the opposite sex. Strip searches are permissible only when it is necessary to maintain the security of the facility, and should be based on probable cause.

It is important for booking officers to properly record and secure prisoners' property. This includes completing a form used to describe the prisoner's possessions and inventorying common articles such as clothing, wallet, jewelry, keys, and so on. These items should be recorded and described as specifically as possible. The booking officer should check to see if the prisoner has an impounded vehicle. If so, vehicle data should be noted in the record as well. Prisoners should sign the form to acknowledge that the inventory is true and correct upon completion of the inventory.

Booking officers should make a detailed account of the prisoner's personal data, including their name; nickname(s); aliases; race; sex; age; date of birth; height; weight; color of hair; color of eyes; complexion; tattoos, scars, marks, and/or deformities; residence address; city and state of residence; driver's license number and issuing state; social security number; emergency contact information; occupation; place of employment; marital status and name of spouse; and name(s) of person(s) arrested with and/or known associates.

Recording information related to the arrest is also part of the booking process. This section of the report includes a description of the charge; information pertaining to warrants (if used); the place of the arrest; the date and time of the arrest; the name(s) of the arresting officer(s); the name of the booking officer; the time the prisoner was booked into jail; information pertaining to the name of the complainant (e.g., name and contact information); facts pertaining to the arrest; the names, addresses, and phone numbers of witnesses; the amount of bond; whether or not a *Miranda* warning was given; a record of phone calls granted and to whom; and the name of the prisoner's attorney. It is important that inventorying a suspect's personal property does not become a search for evidence. Officers must obtain a search warrant if they wish to search the suspect's personal property beyond the legal limits allowed during the booking process.

Arrests involving officer and/or suspect injury require the additional steps of calling for medical assistance for treatment, photographing the injuries sustained by the officer and/or suspect, and properly documenting in the report whether or not the injury occurred in the detention facility. The booking process also involves determining if the offender is wanted by another agency and whether the prisoner possesses stolen property. This is an area where technology has greatly assisted law enforcement efforts to link and/or solve crimes. Increased use of technology in law enforcement has enhanced the booking process, as most administrative records are now entered, compared, accessed, and kept electronically (e.g., "Survey of State," 2003; "System Improves," 1997).

Officers sometimes face resistance while booking a suspect. As this formal indoctrination into the criminal justice system can be highly emotional for some suspects, officers should request the assistance of other officers when dealing with uncooperative prisoners. Officers may also be emotionally attached to the situation (e.g., when an arrest involved an accelerated level of force), in which case the booking should be conducted by another officer. Officers must control their emotions and prejudices, and avoid making offensive and/or abusive remarks to the suspect.

Not all arrestees are booked and detained. For simple offenses the booking process is simplified to include only the name of the person arrested; the name of the arresting officer; the date, time, and place of arrest; and the circumstances of the arrest. In some jurisdictions, those arrested for minor offenses are permitted to post a predetermined amount of bail, or are released with a citation requiring them to appear in court at a later date, similar to the citation one receives following a simple traffic law violation. Other options available to police following an arrest include relocating the suspect to the juvenile justice system, or releasing them from the system. On occasion, additional evidence emerges that refutes the probable cause belief upon which the arrest was made. In these instances the arrestee must be released.

DETENTION

Being released is a priority for those detained in a holding cell or lockup, which are typically found in police departments or precinct houses. Holding facilities are typically temporary facilities maintained by police departments. They are similar to jail facilities typically run by county-level officials; however, holding cells generally do not detain those who have been sentenced, only those awaiting court hearings. Individuals arrested and detained spend some time in a holding cell awaiting their initial appearance before a judge. The courts have ruled that detained arrestees must receive a probable cause hearing within 48 hours, otherwise the burden shifts to the government to explain the emergency or extraordinary situation that prevented the arrestee from appearing before a judge.

"Little is known about detention circumstances in police stations. Research has been conducted about detention in jails and prisons, but hardly any research has been conducted about detention in police stations' cellblocks" (Blaauw, Vermunt, & Kerkhof, 1997, p. 45; see also Williams, 1981). The limited attention in this area is surprising, given Williams's (1981, p. 2) suggestion that aside from making decisions to arrest, "the law enforcement agencies in many jurisdictions control another of the major decision points in the criminal justice process. These agencies often have the power to make the detention decision with little input from other criminal justice agencies." Recent incidents resulting in injuries and deaths to suspects in police custody contributed to some departments revisiting their detention practices.

Officers are required to keep arrestees safely in custody until they appear before a magistrate. "The officer may reasonably restrain the person to prevent escape and may even confine the person in a jail or other suitable place. Handcuffs may be used at the officer's discretion, depending on" a variety of factors including the arrestee's reputation and record for violence (Ferdico, 1996, pp. 147–148). Officers are responsible for the health and safety of the arrestee, and should seek medical assistance if necessary. Any unnecessary force or the failure to prevent the unnecessary use of force by others could result in the officer(s) being subject to civil liability.

CHARGING

The arresting officer typically consults with supervisors, investigators, and/or the district attorney regarding the criminal charge(s) to be filed while the arrestee is being processed by the booking officer. Neubauer (2005) notes that, for the purposes of efficiency, prosecutors possess the legal authority to dictate the charging process (which was the recommendation of the National Advisory Commission on Criminal Justice Standards and Goals [1973]), although some prosecutors choose to share this power with police officers. In some urban areas, assistant prosecutors are available 24 hours a day for consultation with law enforcement regarding the decision to formally file charges. It is possible, after reviewing a case, that the prosecutor sees no need to file formal charges, in which case the suspect is released. Officers may rearrest the suspect for the same offense should they have probable cause and further evidence to make an arrest.

Prosecutors maintain a great deal of discretion, particularly with regard to charging. Several factors influence prosecutorial decisions in filing charges. The seriousness of the offense, the relationship between the suspect and offender, the criminal history of the suspect, and public concern/media attention could influence a prosecutor's decision to file charges. Prosecutors may decide *not* to file charges for several reasons. For instance, not having enough resources to prosecute a case or a lack of evidence to successfully go forward with a case would lead prosecutors to drop charges. Prosecutors may feel public opinion does not support charging a particular offender, in which case they may not prosecute. Similarly, prosecutors may feel the potential penalty is too severe for the crime, so they drop the case or reduce the charges. Plea bargaining is also an option for prosecutors, for instance, when a prosecutor foregoes filing charges if the suspect receives substance abuse treatment.

The interaction between the arresting officer and the prosecutor highlights a key link prosecutors serve between police and the courts, and the great deal of discretion maintained by both police officers and prosecutors. For instance, the police usually have the discretion to charge or not charge a suspect following their arrest, although the amount of officer discretion decreases as the seriousness of the offense increases. Prosecutors, who could be considered the gatekeepers of the American court system, maintain similar discretionary powers, although in most instances the prosecutor makes the final decision regarding whether or not a suspect should be prosecuted (del Carmen, 2004).

Decisions regarding whether or not to prosecute and the charges to be filed are influenced by a series of exchange relations between prosecutors and participants in criminal case processing, including defense attorneys, judges, and police officers (e.g., Cole, 1970). Cole (1970, p. 342) points out that decisions to prosecute are not made at one particular point, instead "the prosecuting attorney has a number of options he may employ during various stages of the proceedings. But the prosecutor is able to exercise his discretionary powers only within the network of exchange relationships." He adds that "The police, court congestion, organizational strains, and community pressures are among the factors that influence prosecutorial behavior" (p. 342).

Interaction between police and prosecutors is important for several reasons, including the need for officers to understand the level of evidence required for a prosecutor to pursue a case. Officers do not wish to make arrests only to have a prosecutor drop charges. "Police departments resist prosecutorial control over the charging decision because they see case rejections as an implicit criticism of the arresting officer for making a 'wrong' arrest" (Neubauer, 2005, p. 224). Individual officers and police departments in general differ in the quality of evidence they bring to prosecutors. Accordingly, the percentage of cases in which a prosecutor files charges differs among departments and according to arresting officers.

Although by law prosecutors should file charges whenever feasible, they've maintained a great deal of discretion and limited accountability for their decision making. For instance, Neubauer (2005, p. 224) notes the absence of "legislative or judicial standards governing which cases merit prosecution and which should be declined," adding that "if a prosecutor refuses to file charges, no review of this decision is possible; courts have consistently refused to order a prosecutor to proceed with a case" (p. 224).

Prosecutors prepare a charging document if they recognize an offense as chargeable. There are three primary types of charging documents: a complaint, an information, and an indictment. An information is the charging document resulting from a preliminary hearing, while an indictment is filed when a grand jury finds probable cause to move forward with case processing. The filing of an indictment or information pertains only to felony cases. With regard to misdemeanors or ordinance violations, prosecutors in many jurisdictions file a complaint, which is a charge that an offense has been committed by a particular person. Complaints require support by oath or affirmation of the victim or arresting officer.

WRAP-UP

The booking and charging stages of criminal case processing demonstrate how criminal justice personnel work as a system in that law enforcement and the courts interact closely. For instance, following an arrest the police process the suspect and turn the case over to prosecutors who decide whether or not to file charges. Charging could not occur without input from the arresting officer. As noted by Fagin (2003, p. 55), "Booking is the procedure that acts as the transition point for moving the arrested person from the police department into the jurisdiction of the court."

Booking and charging have notably different levels of significance in criminal case processing. Booking largely involves the construction of an administrative record of the defendant. Charging, on the other hand, is a significant step that impacts the suspect's processing and disposition. To suspects, charging is far more important than booking. Detention is also more significant than booking to suspects, simply because being detained disrupts lives and makes preparing a defense more difficult.

Point–Counterpoint

Plea bargaining is essential in today's criminal justice system. However, offering "deals" is seen by some as distorting justice. As a result, prosecutors sometimes overcharge suspects knowing that any plea bargain will result in reduced charges, meaning that suspects will ultimately be charged with something akin to the original, "preinflated" charge. *Should prosecutors overcharge suspects?*

Yes: Plea bargaining is the reason our criminal justice system functions. As such, prosecutors must keep in mind various interests and the principles of justice when they face the difficult task of distinguishing acceptable plea proposals from unacceptable ones. Prosecutors face criticism for agreeing to pleas that sometimes permit suspects to admit to something less serious than the crime with which they're charged. They may be viewed as being "too soft." Overcharging provides leverage for prosecutors; it gives them bargaining power and enables them to recognize the principles of justice and serve the public's interests. Overcharging addresses a primary criticism of plea bargaining, as some recognize plea agreements as distorting justice in the sense that an offender is not being charged with the crime they committed. From a utilitarian perspective, overcharging benefits victims, the public, the courts, and prosecutors. The only one who doesn't benefit is the offender. This, to many people, is justice.

No: Overcharging cannot be recognized as justice regardless of any rationalizations. While some may criticize plea bargaining on the grounds that it encourages prosecutors to offer sweetened deals for some who don't deserve them, we must remember that prosecutors are *not* required to enter into plea negotiations. If prosecutors feel plea bargains distort justice then they ought to go to trial in each case, not add unwarranted charges. Adding charges against particular suspects to counter the effects of plea bargaining goes against the principles of justice. The idea of plea bargaining is to encourage suspects to enter a guilty plea with the intent to offer some reward for their cooperation. Penalizing those who choose to plea bargain by overcharging contradicts the nature of plea agreements, and has the potential to result in increasingly overcrowded courts.

SUGGESTED READING

Blaauw, E., Vermunt, R., & Kerkhof, A. (1997). Detention circumstances in police stations: Towards setting the standards. *Policing and Society, 7,* pp. 45–69.

Garipoli, M. A. (2001). Offender identification and central booking project integrates three technologies. *The Police Chief, 68*(10), pp. 108–110.

Gottfredson, M. R., & Gottfredson, D. M. (1988). *Decision making in criminal justice: Toward the rational exercise of discretion* (2nd ed.). New York: Plenum Press.

Spears, J. W., & Spohn, C. C. (1997). The effect of evidence factors and victim characteristics on prosecutors' charging decisions in sexual assault cases. *Justice Quarterly, 14*(3), pp. 501–524.

Williams, M. R. (2003). The effect of pretrial detention on imprisonment decisions. *Criminal Justice Review, 28*(3), pp. 299–316.

CRITICAL THINKING EXERCISES

1. Interaction between the prosecution and police during charging was identified as an example of the police and courts working in a system-like manner. Design and describe a criminal justice system in which the three components (police, courts, and corrections) are administered under one agency.

Would this reorganization result in a more or less effective criminal justice system than is currently in place? Why or why not?

2. Do you feel suspect information collected during the booking process should be made available to the general public? Does your opinion change depending on whether or not the suspect is ultimately convicted?

3. Discuss the pros and cons of revising charging practices and having the charging decision made as a group consisting of the arresting officer, the prosecutor, and the victim. Should we include the suspect? What would be the pros and cons of including suspects in the charging decision-making process?

SHORT ESSAY QUESTIONS

1. How has and how could technology better assist the booking process?

2. Describe the relationship between the police and courts during the charging stage of criminal case processing. In what ways do they work together?

3. What is inventoried and documented during booking?

4. What factors influence prosecutorial decisions to charge a suspect?

5. What steps are taken at booking and in detention to prevent violent confrontations?

PROSECUTION AND PRETRIAL PROCEDURES

5 INITIAL APPEARANCE

James was escorted to the courthouse for his initial appearance before a judge after spending a night in a police detention cell. He was informed by the judge that he was being charged with armed robbery in connection with the robbery of Jane Dahlman (detectives were unable to connect James with the recent robberies in the area). He was then advised of his rights and given the opportunity to retain his lawyer or to have a different one represent him. Like many in the criminal justice system, James did not have the resources to maintain private counsel, so he requested state-funded representation. James was granted pretrial release after he paid a $5,000 bail bond at his initial appearance. He hired a bonding agency to post his bail, which required him to pay the bonding agency 10% of his bail, or $500. James was able to pay the $500 for his release; however, he is now accountable to the bonding agency for the full amount of his bond ($5,000) if he fails to appear at his court hearings.

CASE PROCESSING AND THE INITIAL APPEARANCE

There is a notable difference in how felony and misdemeanor cases are processed. Criminal justice systems devote much less attention to misdemeanors than felonies simply because the consequences and harms posed by misdemeanors are less severe than they are for felonies. Those charged with felonies are much more likely to be taken into custody than those charged with misdemeanors, and felony defendants face additional pretrial activities not required for those charged with misdemeanors. For instance, the initial appearance for felony defendants largely represents a "formality" as defendants are not permitted to enter a plea. Those charged with a felony are not permitted to enter a plea at the initial appearance because the hearing takes place in a court of limited jurisdiction, which does not maintain the authority to accept a plea. In contrast, roughly 75% of those charged with a misdemeanor enter a guilty plea at the initial appearance and are sentenced immediately (Neubauer, 2005).

When dealing with minor offenses and/or those in which a simple citation was issued, magistrates may conduct a summary trial and sentence the offender at the initial appearance. Summary trials conclude the defendant's involvement in the courts, as no further case processing is required. Magistrates may also dismiss a case should they determine that the available evidence is insufficient to warrant further processing. The initial appearance is typically the first time a defendant comes into contact with an officer of the court.

The initial appearance takes a more formal approach for felony defendants. The initial appearance, also referred to as the "first appearance" or "magistrate's review," involves bringing defendants before a judge for the purposes of (1) providing them formal notice of the charges against them; (2) advising them of their rights; (3) giving them the right to retain a lawyer or to have one appointed to represent them; and (4) considering the possibility of pretrial release. Felony defendants are also informed of the upcoming courtroom activities at the initial appearance. Appearances involving unruly, intoxicated, and/or uncooperative suspects may result in the court proceeding with the hearing absent the defendant (Schmalleger, 2005).

The initial appearance may also involve a probable cause, or *Gerstein* hearing. These hearings are sometimes held separately as they do not require the presence of the defendant. Probable cause hearings are required in cases involving a warrantless arrest, simply because such arrests do not require prior judicial determination of probable cause. During a probable cause hearing a judicial officer typically examines police reports to assess whether probable cause supported the arrest. They focus on whether at the time of the arrest the arresting officer had reason to believe that a crime had been, or was being, committed, and that the defendant was the person who had (or was about to) commit it. The suspect is released should no probable cause exist.

Defendants taken into custody have the right to appear before a judge within 48 hours of their arrest. The U.S. Supreme Court ruled in the 1943 case *McNabb v. U.S.* that any confessions made after an unreasonable delay between a defendant's arrest and initial court appearance would be inadmissible. Following the decision in *McNabb,* 48 hours became the standard maximum amount of time a defendant should wait between their arrest and initial appearance (Schmalleger, 2005).

In practice, the initial appearance is typically brief in duration primarily because little is known about the case at this point in the proceedings. The hearing occurs soon after arrest so court officials typically know very little about what transpired. The initial appearance is not a fact-finding, or probable cause, hearing, and the defendant does not have the right to present a defense at this point. Yet, despite the nonadversarial nature of the initial appearance, suspects sometimes state their side of the story at this stage, which results in the judge or the suspect's attorney cautioning them that such information could be used against them (Neubauer, 2005). Those requiring state-provided representation are often accompanied to the initial appearance by an assistant from the government, who monitors activities and provides legal advice. Those retaining private counsel are accompanied by their attorney.

Prosecutors play a significant role throughout criminal case processing. At the initial appearance prosecutors ensure that defendants are aware of the charges against them, and participate in bail discussions. Perhaps the most significant prosecutorial power at this stage is the ability to draft a *nolle prosequi,* which notes that the government is foregoing prosecution of the particular case. Should this occur the defendant is released from the system.

NOTICE OF CHARGES AND ADVISING DEFENDANTS OF THEIR RIGHTS

Due process protections mandate that defendants are informed of, and granted, several rights at the initial appearance. Among other things, the Sixth Amendment states that defendants have the right to know the charges filed against them. One must keep in mind the discretion maintained by prosecutors in filing charges. The defendant at this point, if they are indeed guilty of the offense, is aware of the actions that took place (i.e., the offense); however, the charges filed by the prosecutor are often based on input from others. In turn, the charge may or may not be correct, resulting in some offenders being charged with a more or less severe offense than they deserve. It is during the initial appearance that defendants become aware of the charges formally filed against them. Defendants are also notified of their right to counsel, as provided in the Sixth Amendment, which is perhaps the most significant right provided to defendants at the initial appearance.

Defendants are provided the right to counsel in criminal prosecutions in which the possibility of incarceration, regardless of length of time, exists (*Argersinger v. Hamlin*, 1972). This right protects defendants who do not have the financial resources (i.e., indigent defendants) to be represented in court. Territo, Halsted, and Bromley (2004) note that judges in many jurisdictions have the discretion to provide defendants assistance other than counsel, for example, they may appoint medical experts or investigators to an indigent case. Furthermore, defendants at a joint trial may be represented by only one lawyer, in essence sharing the court-appointed representation. Defendants are entitled to representation at any critical stage of criminal case processing, although they are not entitled to counsel during probation and parole revocation hearings, or during discretionary appellate hearings (Territo et al., 2004). Defendants do have the right to represent themselves in court, although they must be advised of their rights and "be competent to intelligently and voluntarily abandon the right" (Territo et al., 2004, p. 127).

COUNSEL AND THE INITIAL APPEARANCE

Most defendants lack the financial means to secure private counsel. Research on felony defendants in large state courts found that about 18% of those who enter the criminal justice system hire a private attorney, leaving the other 82% to rely on state-provided representation (Harlow, 2000). There is debate regarding the quality and overall effectiveness of state-provided representation, as it is suggested that those represented by private counsel maintain an advantage over those receiving state-appointed representation. The concern centers not around the competency of those representing the indigent; instead, the criticism concerns the limited resources and large caseloads often maintained by public defenders and others representing the poor. Plea bargains are encouraged when attorneys do not have adequate resources to devote to each case. There is some evidence, however, that those representing the indigent generally are as successful as private counsel (Hanson & Ostrom, 2002).

Magistrates will note whether a defendant is represented by counsel at the initial appearance. Should the defendant note their lack of financial means to secure representation, the magistrate will inquire into the defendant's financial status in what is typically known as an indigency hearing. Specific standards must be met to demonstrate indigency in some courts. "In most courts, however, it is not necessary to establish total destitution" (Territo et al., 2004, p. 127). If it is determined that the defendant is indeed indigent, the magistrate will require the defendant to sign an affidavit noting their impoverishment (Territo et al., 2004). Representation at this point will be provided by the State.

State-provided representation exists in three forms: public defenders, assigned counsel, and contract systems. Public defenders are salaried staff that provide indigent representation through a public or private nonprofit agency. Put simply, their primary task as practicing attorneys is to represent the indigent. Assigned counsel involves the appointment of indigent representation from a list of private practicing attorneys. Courts using assigned counsel systems select names from a list of practicing attorneys who are summoned to represent indigent defendants. The attorneys are reimbursed by the State for their work. Contract systems involve nonsalaried groups contracting with the State to provide representation for indigent defendants. For instance, a private law firm may contract with the government to accept all indigent cases for a specified period at a set financial cost.

Research suggests that the 4.2 million cases requiring indigent representation in the United States' 100 most populous counties in 1999 cost an estimated $1.2 billion, with most of these funds (73%) spent on public defender programs. Public defenders assumed roughly 82% of the indigent cases, followed by assigned counsel (15%) and contract attorneys (3%) (DeFrances & Litras, 2000). To address the limitations of current methods of indigent representation, some jurisdictions adopted mixed systems in which both public defenders and private attorneys are used. Law school students and prepaid legal service programs also provide assistance for the indigent (Senna & Siegel, 2002). Furthermore, some attorneys provide indigent defense *pro bono,* or on a volunteer basis.

PRETRIAL RELEASE

Suspects are not guaranteed pretrial release, although most of the accused are released prior to trial. Those charged with serious crimes, individuals believed to be a danger to society, or those deemed a flight risk are typically detained in jail until trial in what is called pretrial detention. Many jurisdictions use pretrial services programs, or early intervention programs, to gather and present information about defendants and release options, and to supervise defendants released from custody during the pretrial phase (Mahoney, Beaudin, Carver, Ryan, & Hoffman, 2001).

Setting bail is one of the most significant aspects of the initial appearance. In some cases bail is determined and temporary release is granted for defendants at the booking phase. The decision to detain or release defendants is typically made by a judge or an appointed hearing officer. The process initially involves deciding whether to grant the defendant pretrial release at all. Should the defendant be deemed worthy of release, the judge/officer will consider what type of release is appropriate. Judges and officers consider a number of factors in their decision to release, including the seriousness of the current charge; the defendant's prior record; background information about the defendant (e.g., community and family ties, employment status, substance abuse problems, etc.); and information concerning available supervisory options if the defendant is released (Schmalleger, 2005).

Primary concerns regarding pretrial release include pretrial crime and failure to appear for trial. However, Jackson (1987) found that serious pretrial crime was committed infrequently by those on pretrial release. His findings concur with existing research, which, as noted by Jackson, suggests that "arrests of pretrial releasees for serious crimes are relatively infrequent . . . ; the ability to accurately predict pretrial crime . . . is very poor; and . . . the level of pretrial crime correlates positively with time on release" (p. 307). Accordingly, Gottfredson and Gottfredson (1988, p. 98) note, "the available studies demonstrate the difficulty of achievement of either of the predominantly expressed goals of the pretrial release decision, both of which require predictions—failure to appear for trial and pretrial crime." They suggest the "errors involved in such predictions are very large" (p. 98), with evidence pointing to the overprediction of both failure to appear and pretrial crime. They add, however, that there is room for improvement in the prediction process.

Bail, the most common form of pretrial release, is provided by the Eighth Amendment, which states, among other things, that "excessive bail shall not be required." Despite this clause and the goals of bail (to ensure that defendants will return to court and to prevent the unnecessary incarceration of unconvicted suspects), there are instances when bail is denied. For instance, judges may deny pretrial release to those who: (1) are accused of a heinous offense, (2) pose a substantial threat to society, and (3) pose a flight risk. In practice, most cases do not meet these requirements and some form of pretrial release is granted. Bail is an agreement or pledge that the defendant will return to court. Failure to abide by the terms of the agreement without a sufficient justification results in bail forfeiture and the defendant deemed a fugitive from justice. A bench warrant is then issued for the defendant's arrest and additional charges are filed for this newly committed offense.

Bail bonds typically involve cash deposits, but can come in the form of property or other valuables. Many defendants do not have the financial means to pay bail, thus they rely on the services of a bail bonding agency, which posts the defendant's bail for a 10–15% surcharge to the defendant (otherwise known as surety bond). However, several states passed legislation outlawing for-profit bonding, replacing them with state-operated pretrial services.

Aside from posting financial bail, states and the federal government make other options available for defendants to secure pretrial release. These alternatives include release on recognizance (a written agreement that the accused will return to court); property bonds (property offered in lieu of cash [e.g., house, car]); deposit bail (the defendant pays a percentage of the bail yet is responsible for the full amount if they don't return to court); conditional release (the defendant must abide by specific conditions [e.g., substance abuse counseling]); third-party custody (the court assigns the defendant to a third party who becomes responsible for the defendant's presence in court); and unsecured bonds, which require no monetary payment, although defendants are responsible for the full amount should they fail to return to court.

Rainville and Reaves (2003) found that about 62% of felony defendants in the 75 largest U.S. counties were released prior to the disposition of their case. Of the 38% of defendants who remained detained until disposition, only about 7% were denied bail, 46% of whom were charged with murder. Overall, those charged with violent offenses were least likely to be released (56%), while those charged with public-order offenses were most likely to be released (66%).

Rainville and Reaves (2003) also found that a bail amount was set for 63% of felony defendants, while 30% were granted nonfinancial release. The remaining 7% were held without bail, and a very small percentage (less than .5%) were granted emergency release. Defendants charged with violent offenses had their bail set at notably higher levels than those charged with other offenses. Surety bonds were most often used by those released on financial bail, while release on recognizance was the most commonly issued type of nonfinancial release. Finally, Rainville and Reaves found that of those released prior to case disposition, half were released within one day of their arrest, and 78% were released within one week.

It is well established that decisions regarding pretrial release impact a defendant's outcome in the criminal justice system. In particular, pretrial detention may encourage defendants to plea bargain, and those who are detained prior to trial are more likely to be convicted and receive more punitive sentences, perhaps because of their inability to adequately prepare their case (Gottfredson & Gottfredson, 1988). There is evidence, however, that pretrial detention may not have a major effect on whether a defendant is convicted (e.g., Goldkamp, 1979).

Research on extralegal variables affecting bail outcomes suggests that judges consider gender in determining *the amount of bail* for particular types of cases, and both race and gender appear to affect *the likelihood of pretrial release* (Katz & Spohn, 1995). Other research suggests that individuals who are married and/or have dependants are less likely than their counterparts to be detained prior to trial (Daly, 1987).

WRAP-UP

The initial appearance is the first step in a series of pretrial procedures that play an integral role in criminal case processing. While most of us are familiar with many steps of case processing through popular culture and media coverage, it is argued that the public knows very little, relatively speaking, about what happens following arrest and prior to trial. In discussing the significance of pretrial procedures, Feeley (1979, p. 241) argues that "The real punishment for many people is the pretrial process itself; that is why criminally accused invoke so few of the adversarial options available to them." He adds that cumbersome criminal case processing encourages the accused to limit their involvement with the criminal justice system, for instance, by waiving their right to trial and engaging in plea negotiations.

Our case study of James's experience in the criminal justice system exemplifies the path taken by many who enter the system. At his initial appearance, James was informed of his legal rights, was provided the opportunity to post bail, and was informed of the charges against him. Had James been charged with a misdemeanor instead of a felony, it is likely he would have entered a plea at this point and a verdict would be announced. Depending on the verdict, James would've either exited the criminal justice system or been sentenced. James, unable to post bail, relied on the services of a bonding agency and will be charged a fee for their services. Following the initial appearance, James's case will be turned over to a grand jury.

Point–Counterpoint

Some question the ethical and practical issues of enabling defendants to obtain pretrial release via the assistance of private bonding agencies. In fact, the 1984 Federal Bail Reform Act threatened the existence of bonding agencies by granting federal judges power to detain those deemed a threat to society. This act was passed despite the integral role of bonding agencies in the criminal justice system. *Should defendants be granted the opportunity to obtain pretrial release via the assistance of private bonding agencies?*

Yes: Bail bond agencies provide an invaluable service to the criminal justice system. Assisting the courts with ensuring that defendants return for court proceedings and managing jail populations are among the benefits of allowing bonding agencies to provide pretrial release for those who cannot afford it. From an efficiency and financial standpoint, the use of bonding agencies makes great sense in that the criminal justice system can more effectively use the resources that would otherwise be directed toward tracking individuals who fail to appear in court. Similarly, the problem of jail overcrowding would be much worse if bonding agencies did not facilitate the release of defendants.

No: Aside from the questionable practices used by bail bondsmen to track those who flee, and the outdated legislation granting bail enforcement agents fewer legal restrictions than police, "(b)ail bondsmen have been linked to many corrupt practices" (Shelden & Brown, 2003, p. 216). Among the concerns are bonding agencies bribing criminal justice officials to inflate bail amounts and offering kickbacks to judges who decline to collect on outstanding sureties. Furthermore, questions of justice and fairness arise considering the power of bonding agencies to determine who is released from jail and who remains detained. Such unsavory practices and the questionable appropriateness of privately secured bail led several states and all common-law countries to abolish bail bonding for profit as an option.

SUGGESTED READING

Goldkamp, J. (1979). *Two classes of accused: A study of bail and detention in America.* Cambridge, MA: Ballinger.

Goldkamp, J. S., & Gottfredson, M. (1979). Bail decision making and pretrial detention: Surfacing judicial policy. *Law and Human Behavior, 3,* pp. 227–249.

Gottfredson, M. R., & Gottfredson, D. M. (1988). *Decision making in criminal justice: Toward the rational exercise of discretion* (2nd ed.). New York: Plenum Press.

Jackson, P. G. (1987). The impact of pretrial preventive detention. *Justice System Journal, 12*(3), pp. 305–334.

Johnson, B. R., & Warchol, G. L. (2003). Bail agents and bounty hunters: Adversaries or allies of the justice system. *American Journal of Criminal Justice, 27*(2), pp. 145–165.

CRITICAL THINKING EXERCISES

1. Assume you're given the role of overhauling your city's indigent defense system. Claims of inadequate representation and lack of resources plague your public defender's office. How would you change things?

2. Suppose a wealthy man and an indigent man, both with no criminal backgrounds, commit the same offense. Should they each be required to post the same amount of cash bail? Why or why not?

3. Should defendants be granted the right to decline their right to counsel? Should they be permitted to defend themselves in court? What are the benefits of defending one's self in court? What are some of the drawbacks?

SHORT ESSAY QUESTIONS

1. What takes place at the initial appearance? What rights are provided to defendants at this stage?

2. How does case processing differ between misdemeanors and felonies with regard to the initial appearance?

3. Discuss the three types of representation offered to indigent defendants. What are the benefits and limitations of each approach?

4. What factors are considered by court officials in the decision to grant a defendant pretrial release?

5. Aside from cash bail, what are the various types of pretrial release?

6

PRELIMINARY AND GRAND JURY HEARINGS

The State in which James is accused of robbing Jane uses a grand jury to determine whether probable cause exists to believe a crime was committed and the accused (in our case, James) should stand trial. Following the testimony of witnesses presented by the prosecution (Cedric and technicians from the crime lab who examined the cigarette lighter for fingerprints), the grand jury met in closed hearings on James's case and issued an indictment. The indictment noted their probable cause belief that James was responsible for the crime. Neither James nor his attorney were permitted to attend the hearing, nor were they permitted to offer evidence. The grand jury quickly indicted James, as it was very clear to them that there was probable cause to believe a crime was committed and that James was responsible. The indictment makes James's case typical of most others that go before a grand jury. However, unless he plea bargains, James's case will be atypical of most criminal cases in that he will go to trial.

To this point James has proceeded directly through the criminal justice system. We must remember that at any point James may be dismissed from the system (e.g., through the introduction or loss of crucial evidence), or James may plea bargain. A plea bargain would involve James admitting guilt in return for some favor, most likely a less punitive sentence than he presently faces (which, among other benefits to the justice system, would reduce the resources needed to prosecute James). Plea bargains require an agreement between the prosecution and defense and must be approved by a judge. Research on felony adjudication in the 75 largest U.S. counties suggests about 64% of felony defendants whose cases were processed within one year were convicted of either a felony or a misdemeanor, with 95% of the dispositions the result of a plea bargain (Rainville & Reaves, 2003). The high percentage of plea bargains occurs despite defendants having no constitutional right to plea agreements. As noted, James's case will be atypical of most criminal cases if he chooses to go to trial.

Felonies are serious crimes that are punishable, in the United States, by a year in prison. Accordingly, felony cases include additional steps not found in misdemeanor case processing. These steps are primarily designed to ensure that a crime has indeed taken place and the defendant should stand trial for the crime. Preliminary hearings and grand jury hearings are used in U.S. courts to examine evidence and help ensure that all that has occurred in case processing to this point is just. These two types of hearings differ in the manner in which they are conducted, yet they share the same aforementioned goals. Justification for these hearings stems from the legal requirement that nobody can be required to respond to criminal charges absent an approved group's determination that sufficient evidence exists to bring the defendant to trial (Anderson, 1957).

The events shift from a nonadversarial approach to an adversarial one at this stage in case processing. Evidence is introduced in both the preliminary hearing and grand jury hearing, and cases are further developed. Much of the input at this stage is provided by the State, as it is the prosecution's task to demonstrate guilt. The required level of proof in these hearings is probable cause, much less than the required "proof beyond a reasonable doubt" required in jury trials. Accordingly, few cases are rejected from the system at this stage.

The preliminary hearing can be considered an abbreviated trial. Sometimes referred to as a "bindover hearing," "a probable cause hearing," or a "preliminary examination," the preliminary hearing primarily consists of the prosecution presenting evidence before a judge with the intent to demonstrate probable cause that a crime was committed and the defendant should be charged. The preliminary hearing is open to the public. A grand jury hearing maintains the same goals, although the means of attaining those goals are different. A grand jury consists of laypersons (similar to trial juries) weighing evidence in closed hearings. An indictment is issued if a grand jury finds probable cause to believe that a crime was committed and the defendant should be charged. The grand jury also has investigative powers and can initiate and conduct its own investigation without police intervention.

CASE PROCESSING AND THE PRELIMINARY HEARING

A preliminary hearing may follow the initial appearance. The hearing is primarily designed to protect defendants from unjust prosecution. Keeping this goal in mind, at the preliminary hearing the prosecution makes the case that a crime was committed and the defendant should be held accountable. The judge's role at the preliminary hearing is to preside over the hearing and offer an opinion regarding the need for further case processing. In doing so, judges consider the evidence being presented, examine the legality of the defendant's arrest and any searches relating to the arrest, and assess the bail that may have been set at the initial appearance. Depending on their level of authority, judges may be permitted to raise or lower the bail amount. In some jurisdictions the preliminary hearing is also the venue for some pretrial motions to exclude evidence (Territo et al., 2004).

The defendant and their representation are present for the preliminary hearing, with both sides swearing in and presenting evidence. Strategically, both sides may introduce witnesses who may be unable to attend a trial with the intent to preserve their input, as long as the other side has the opportunity to cross-examine the witness. The preliminary hearing, which typically occurs in a lower court, is the first stage during criminal case processing in which someone other than law enforcement hears the defendant's case.

Although the preliminary hearing could be considered an abbreviated trial, a jury does not participate in the hearing. Judges make the determination regarding whether to hold defendants for trial. The prosecution must present evidence at the preliminary hearing primarily because they have the burden of proof. Defendants have the right to present evidence and fully participate in the hearing, although they seldom offer evidence (Territo et al., 2004). The defense generally does not have the right to cross-examine witnesses, although some jurisdictions and judges will permit the defense to ask questions (Gilboy, 1984). Defendants are not required to enter a plea at the preliminary hearing.

The preliminary hearing can be vital to case outcome in several ways. For instance, an important feature of the preliminary hearing is the opportunity for the defense to discover the nature or direction of the prosecution's case or strategy. The prosecution does not have to present its entire case at this time, just enough to demonstrate probable cause. Defense attorneys may want to use the preliminary hearing to demonstrate to their client the significance of their case (Neubauer, 2005), and the extra time provided by the preliminary hearing helps defense attorneys prepare their case (Shelden & Brown, 2003). Defendants have the right to waive the preliminary hearing, and may wish to do so if they decide to plead guilty or seek to avoid negative publicity that might emerge from the hearing (Territo et al., 2004). Approval from the judge and prosecution is required to waive a preliminary hearing. Waiving the preliminary hearing benefits the prosecution, which doesn't have to expose its case; however, prosecutors may wish to conduct a preliminary hearing for the purposes of having on record the testimony of witnesses who may not be available at the trial stage. Furthermore, the preliminary hearing is the only procedure to consider the existence of probable cause in states with no grand jury provisions.

Preliminary hearings are almost never held in some jurisdictions that permit them. For instance, most cases at the federal level (which requires a grand jury hearing) are initiated with a grand jury indictment, which then leads to an arrest, rendering no need for a preliminary hearing. In other words, probable cause was established by a grand jury prior to arrest, eliminating the need for a preliminary hearing. Even when there is an arrest prior to a grand jury hearing, federal prosecutors will seek a grand jury indictment prior to the 10-day requirement for a preliminary hearing (Neubauer, 1999).

Following the preliminary hearing, judges may bind over the defendant to trial or a grand jury (depending on procedure), reduce the charges (which is an option in most states), or dismiss the accused should the judge find no probable cause. Few cases are dismissed at the preliminary hearing, simply because establishing probable cause is not overly difficult at this stage. Judges often find that probable cause exists at the preliminary hearing and order the suspect held for further case processing. In most cases bound over for trial, prosecutors file an information, the charging document used in preliminary hearings, with the superior court. The time permitted to file a case varies among jurisdictions, although 15 days from the preliminary hearing is typical (Territo et al., 2004).

The significance and duration of preliminary hearings vary by jurisdiction, although the intent of the hearings remains constant. In some courts the hearing may last for hours, while in others they may be short in duration and recognized as a perfunctory step in which probable cause is almost always found (Neubauer, 2005).

In her study of the prosecutor's discretionary use of grand juries, Gilboy (1984) found that being discharged following a preliminary or grand jury hearing may not be the end of the defendant's prosecution. In states that provide the option of a grand jury, prosecutors can take a case directly to a grand jury should a judge at the preliminary hearing find no probable cause to further process the defendant. Or, prosecutors may reinitiate prosecution and refile charges at a second preliminary hearing. Refiling charges following a judge or grand jury's decision to discharge a defendant is not considered "double jeopardy," which generally does not apply until a trial begins (Gilboy, 1984).

Some states use preliminary hearings as a primary step to trial, while others use it to bind over the defendant to a grand jury. Furthermore, some states refer defendants solely to the grand jury, while others have the option of bypassing the preliminary hearing and referring the case directly to a grand jury (Senna & Siegel, 2002). Most states used a preliminary hearing in felony cases as of the late 1990s.

CASE PROCESSING AND THE GRAND JURY

Similar to preliminary hearings, grand jury hearings are used to assess whether enough evidence exists to justify a felony trial. Unless waived by the defendant, a grand jury indictment is required for felony prosecutions in the federal system and about one-third of state court systems, although its use in American criminal justice is diminishing. In cases where a decision was already made at a preliminary hearing, the grand jury can reject or reinstate prosecution; it is not bound by the decision rendered at the preliminary hearing.

The Fifth Amendment states that all citizens are guaranteed the right to indictment by a grand jury, although the 1884 Supreme Court case *Hurtado v. California* declared that states were not required to abide by this law. In turn, states are divided in the use of grand juries. As noted by Worrall and Hemmens (2005, p. 42), "Fewer than half the states require an indictment; 12 states require indictment by a grand jury only for felonies, while 3 states require indictment by a grand jury only for capital offenses." They add, "Four states require indictment by a grand jury for all felonies and misdemeanors" (p. 42).

The grand jury is composed of a group of private citizens selected to review felony cases. Their term on a grand jury can last anywhere from one to several months, although they generally serve for no more than 3 months. Grand juries in the midst of a major and/or intense investigation may have their time extended by the court (Neubauer, 2005). Grand juries generally range in size from 6 to 23 members, although they typically consist of 19 members (Stuckey, Roberson, & Wallace, 2004). They meet in closed sessions and are presented evidence, including witness testimony, photographs, documents, and so on from the prosecution only. Similar to trial juries, grand juries should represent the community conscience, although grand juries do not render a guilty or not guilty verdict. Instead, the grand jury, which is theoretically representative of the community in which it is assembled, assesses the legality of the charges and the processing of defendants.

Selection practices for grand jury members vary by state, with some states choosing jurors at random (e.g., from voting lists) and others permitting judges to offer to the clerk of court the names of potential jurors (Stuckey et al., 2004). Volunteers serve on grand juries in some places. Qualifications to serve on a grand jury include being at least 18 years old, a citizen of the United States, a resident of the jurisdiction for at least one year, and the ability to communicate in English (Senna & Siegel, 2002).

Grand jury hearings also require probable cause as the standard of proof for further case processing. In addition to adjudicating probable cause, grand juries also serve the important function of investigating crimes, and are usually impaneled to investigate political corruption or organized crime (Territo et al., 2004). Senna and Siegel (2002, p. 347) suggest the investigative role of the grand jury is a "valuable and necessary function" whose role should be expanded.

Grand juries issue a bill of indictment, or a *true bill,* if they find probable cause. They issue a *no bill* if they don't find probable cause, and the case is dropped. The case can, however, be brought before another grand jury in some jurisdictions (Bohm & Haley, 2002). Grand juries issue a *presentment* in cases where they find probable cause as a result of their own investigation.

Prosecutorial discretion plays a significant role in jurisdictions using grand juries. In particular, prosecutors play the roles of judge and prosecutor within the grand jury, and are the only legal officers in the room when grand jury members weigh evidence. Furthermore, prosecutors determine what evidence will be shared with the grand jury (Territo et al., 2004), which certainly influences grand jury decisions to indict. Defendants are legally not permitted to be present during grand jury deliberations.

Stuckey and colleagues (2004) cite the importance of the indictment, particularly its role in informing the jury of the charges in the particular case; providing a vehicle for the grand jury to state its decision; serving as an arrest warrant in cases where the defendant is not in custody; and informing defendants of the charges filed against them. The prosecutor prepares the indictment prior to grand jury hearings, leaving the jury to merely sign the statement should they find probable cause to indict.

Grand juries almost always find probable cause to indict defendants (e.g., Worrall & Hemmens, 2005). Neubauer (2005, p. 229) notes: "In short, grand juries generally indict whomever the prosecutor wants indicted" and are sometimes viewed as nothing more than a rubber stamp for the prosecution. Primary reasons behind the high likelihood of indictments include the low level of proof required (probable cause); the inapplicability of the exclusionary rule in grand juries in some jurisdictions; the need for only a half to two-thirds of the votes being required to find probable cause (no unanimity is required) in most states; and because hearsay evidence is usually permissible in grand jury deliberations. The high rate of indictments could also be reflective of effective screening practices on behalf of prosecutors who dismiss cases they believe aren't worthy of grand jury consideration. Suspects in about 80% of cases waive their right to a grand jury hearing simply because of the high rate of indictments and the preference to speed up case processing (Bohm & Haley, 2002).

A unique aspect of the grand jury is the secrecy involved. The criminal justice system seemingly prides itself in being open to the public. The hidden grand jury hearings, however, go against the openness of the system. The reasoning behind the closed grand jury hearings involves a concern to protect those under investigation (who remain innocent until proven guilty) from unwarranted publicity (Neubauer, 2005).

Grand juries are criticized for having a negligible effect on criminal case processing, with some arguing that the costs outweigh the benefits. Senna and Siegel (2002, p. 347) note that "One common complaint is that the grand jury is costly in terms of space, personnel, and money. The members must be selected, notified, sworn, housed, fed, and granted other considerations." They add that the general view is that grand juries should only be summoned in cases in which a community voice is warranted.

DIFFERENCES BETWEEN HEARINGS

Although they share similar goals, preliminary examinations and grand jury proceedings differ in several ways. For instance, an *indictment* is used in grand jury hearings as a formal charging document, while defendants are bound over to a grand jury or trial via an *information* following preliminary hearings. Grand jury hearings are informal, nonadversarial proceedings held in closed sessions in which no judge presides; preliminary hearings are formal, adversarial proceedings open to the public and presided over by a judge. Defendants in most states have no right to counsel, to be present, or to offer evidence at grand jury hearings, although they are given the right to counsel and may be present and offer evidence in a preliminary hearing. Preliminary hearings are designed to more quickly facilitate criminal case processing; it is "a more efficient way to proceed than a grand jury indictment because it eliminates the need to organize a grand jury and present evidence" (Worrall & Hemmens, 2005, p. 42). Finally, grand jury proceedings, unlike preliminary examinations, include the power to investigate crime.

WRAP-UP

The United States' decentralized form of government, which is based on the principles of federalism (or distributing power among different levels of government), results in varied approaches to criminal case processing. Despite the many benefits associated with a decentralized system of justice, the inconsistencies associated with federalism make it difficult to comprehend government practices and behaviors. In discussing the decentralized approach to criminal justice, Neubauer (2005, p. 4) notes: "state governments create local units of government, such as counties and cities. Each of these levels of government is associated with its own array of police, courts, and corrections. This decentralization adds tremendously to the complexity of American criminal justice." It is perhaps within the American court system that the complexity of the system is most evident. For instance, as noted above, some states use preliminary hearings, others use grand juries. Furthermore, the significance and nature of the preliminary and grand jury hearings vary by jurisdiction. In sum, there is no single method of establishing probable cause at this stage of criminal case processing.

Whether a jurisdiction uses a preliminary hearing, a grand jury hearing, or both for felony processing, the goal of this stage of criminal case processing remains the same: to establish probable cause that a crime was committed and that the defendant should be held accountable for the offense. In our case study, James experienced the frustration of many who are impacted by grand jury hearings in that he was not permitted to offer evidence in support of his case. Instead, a prosecutor met in private with a grand jury, which resulted in an indictment, much like most other cases that go before a grand jury. Had James committed his offense in a different state, it is possible that he would have had a preliminary hearing, which at the very least permits the defendant (James) the opportunity to be present while his fate was determined.

Point–Counterpoint

Some suggest grand juries are a relic of historical criminal justice practices that currently consume resources and provide little in return. Others note the strengths of grand juries, including the power to conduct investigations. *Should we abolish the use of grand juries?*

Yes: Grand juries are a holdover from historically idealistic views that common citizens would not be easily influenced by skilled prosecutors. Grand jury decisions are overwhelmingly influenced by prosecutors, and are an unnecessary waste of jury resources. Grand jury hearings result in unnecessary case delay and have a negligible effect on criminal case processing, simply because almost all cases appearing before a grand jury result in an indictment. Originally designed to promote individual rights, grand juries have largely had the opposite effect. Among the concerns are the neglect of due process rights by allowing hearsay evidence; granting the prosecution control over the hearings; not permit-

ting the defense the opportunity to cross-examine witnesses or present evidence; and holding the hearings in closed, secretive sessions.

No: Despite several shortcomings, grand juries serve an incredibly useful purpose in the criminal justice system. Designed to represent the community conscience, grand juries help prevent prosecutorial misconduct, and maintain the invaluable power to initiate their own investigations. The argument that grand juries do nothing more than succumb to prosecutorial wishes is unsubstantiated. Perhaps the high rate of indictments emanating from grand jury hearings is the result of effective prosecutorial case screening. In other words, it is argued that grand juries indict at such a high rate simply because weak cases have already been dismissed by the time a case reaches a grand jury. The closed, secretive approach taken by grand juries is designed to protect the innocent from public scrutiny. Abolish the grand jury system? No, although reforming the system is certainly an option. Perhaps we should use them in a more selective manner.

SUGGESTED READING

Clark, L. (1972). *The grand jury: The use and abuse of political power.* New York: Quadrangle Books.

Deutsch, M. (1984). The improper use of the federal grand jury: An instrument for the internment of political activists. *Journal of Criminal Law and Criminology, 75,* pp. 1159–1189.

Emerson, D. (1983). *Grand jury reform—A review of key issues.* Washington, DC: U.S. Department of Justice, National Institute of Justice.

Gilboy, J. A. (1984, Winter). Prosecutors' discretionary use of the grand jury to initiate or to reinitiate prosecution. *American Bar Foundation Research Journal, 9*(1), pp. 1–81.

Kuckes, N. (2004). The useful, dangerous fiction of grand jury independence. *American Criminal Law Review, 41,* pp. 1–66.

CRITICAL THINKING EXERCISES

1. Discuss why, if you were a felony defendant, you would prefer to have either a grand jury or a preliminary hearing. What are the pros and cons of each?
2. Probable cause is found in just about all preliminary and grand jury hearings. As a result, should we abolish this step? Should we revise this phase of criminal case processing? How can we make it more effective?
3. Discuss why a defendant would waive their right to a preliminary hearing. Are these reasons different from the reasons behind why a defendant would waive their right to a grand jury hearing?

SHORT ESSAY QUESTIONS

1. With regard to grand jury and preliminary hearings, how is felony case processing different from misdemeanor case processing?

2. How is a grand jury hearing different from a preliminary hearing?

3. Discuss why you believe cases in which probable cause was not found in a preliminary hearing should or should not be refiled and prosecuted in another preliminary hearing.

4. What are the arguments for and against the use of a grand jury?

5. What benefits do defendants receive from a preliminary hearing?

ARRAIGNMENT

James was formally arraigned following the grand jury indictment. He was once again informed of the charges against him (armed robbery) and allowed to enter a plea at the arraignment. James and his attorney felt they had a strong defense and entered a "not guilty" plea, which prompted the judge to initiate plans for a trial. At the arraignment, James's attorney entered a pretrial motion to had the case moved to another venue, primarily because of media attention to violent crime in the city where James was being held. The series of robberies was covered heavily by the media, thus James's attorney felt his client would have a better chance of going before an unbiased jury if the case was moved to another location. The judge denied the motion. James's attorney began preparing for the upcoming trial, in part, through applying discovery statutes, which permit the defense to examine the prosecution's evidence. Unlike most defendants, James has no intentions of plea bargaining.

CASE PROCESSING AND THE ARRAIGNMENT

Following the return of an indictment or the filing of an information, the next step in criminal case processing is the arraignment. The arraignment, which is often brief in duration (typically lasting no more than 10–15 minutes), is the final step in criminal case processing prior to trial. The arraignment primarily consists of two significant events: the accused once again being informed of the charges against him or her, and the accused entering a plea. Pretrial motions may be offered at this stage, as attorneys anticipate going to trial. Arraignments are sometimes confused with initial appearances, as both involve defendants entering a plea. One must remember, however, that pleas are entered at the initial appearance in misdemeanor processing and at the arraignment in felony processing.

Defendants are informed of the charges against them, as noted in the information or indictment, at the arraignment. These charges may be different than those initially filed against the defendant, as significant events may have occurred since the prosecution filed charges. The prosecution cannot change the charges that have been filed once the arraignment takes place, which provides the defense the opportunity to prepare their case for trial without concern for new, or altered, charges. Should the prosecution wish to change the charges following the preliminary hearing or grand jury hearing, new charges must be filed and the pretrial processes begin anew. The judge must ensure that defendants understand the charges against them. The defendant is asked to enter a plea after the charges are read and the judge is convinced the defendant is aware of the charges. Defendants who, at this point, have yet to obtain counsel may request that the court provide representation. Judges will ascertain the name and place of residence of defendants, and may confirm the pretrial detention status of the defendant at the arraignment.

In some states the initial appearance is waived and the pretrial processes begin with the arraignment, particularly in cases involving arrests made via an arrest warrant. In these jurisdictions the information gathered and considered in support of the arrest warrant is recognized as sufficient for detaining a defendant prior to arraignment.

Neubauer (2005, p. 11) argues that "Overall, little of importance happens during arraignment; this legal step is somewhat equivalent to the taking of class attendance."

He adds that the arraignment plays a limited role in criminal case processing; it is recognized for indirectly signifying to members of the courtroom workgroup that the defendant is probably guilty. Barkan and Bryjak (2004), however, note that the arraignment does not necessarily signify guilt for all defendants, as one of two possibilities could occur between the arraignment and trial (or guilty plea) that could benefit the defendant: (1) changing circumstances (e.g., uncovering evidence that enhances the defendant's case), and (2) the refusal or inability of prosecutorial witnesses to testify. Judicial decision making regarding pretrial motions could also benefit defendants.

PLEAS

Criminal defendants typically enter one of three pleas in response to the charges filed against them: guilty, not guilty, or *nolo contendere.* Some defendants stand mute, and refuse to respond to the charges. Standing mute is viewed as the defendant's noncooperation with the court and results in the court entering a not guilty plea on behalf of the defendant. Some states permit defendants to plead "not guilty by reason of insanity," which insinuates that the defendant could not be responsible for the charges filed against them as they lacked the mental capacity to understand their actions. States that do not permit this plea require suspects who wish to explain their behavior as the result of mental illness to enter a "not guilty" plea and demonstrate insanity at trial. A handful of states offer a "guilty but mentally ill" plea which requires those who commit a crime while mentally ill to receive psychological treatment followed by prison time, as opposed to merely serving time in a mental treatment facility (for elaboration, see Borum & Fulero, 1999; Palmer & Hazelrigg, 2000). Insanity pleas are rarely used in the courts and few defendants are found insane when the defense is used (McGinley & Pasewark, 1989).

Defendants sometimes plead guilty to the original charges filed against them, while other times they plead guilty to reduced charges following a plea agreement. Pleading guilty results in defendants sacrificing many constitutional protections, thus judges do not always accept guilty pleas. Judges may rule that a "not guilty" plea be entered if it is felt the defendant offered a guilty plea under duress or because he or she lacked knowledge of their situation. Judges must inform those entering a guilty plea of possible sanctions associated with the charges filed against them, including the maximum sentence the defendant may receive. Defendants are sentenced following a guilty plea.

Defendants sometimes plead *nolo contendere,* which essentially means "I do not contest the charges." By entering this plea, which requires consent from the prosecution or the court's permission, the defendant is neither admitting to or denying the charges against them. The legal consequences of a *nolo contendere* plea is the same as a guilty plea, although some defendants prefer *nolo contendere,* an "implied confession" (Barkan & Bryjak, 2004, p. 295), because they can facilitate case processing without admitting guilt. A plea of *nolo contendere,* which is most common in nonserious offenses, is preferable to a guilty plea to some defendants. For instance, defendants are protected from having an admission of guilt used against them in any subsequent civil cases by not entering a guilty plea in a criminal case. A plea of *nolo contendere* also benefits defendants who, often out of principle, may not wish to admit guilt, although they do wish to cooperate with the court and facilitate case processing. Defendants, for example, may disagree with the legality of the law they are accused of violating. *Nolo contendere* pleas are permissible in the federal courts and in the courts of about half of all states, although defendants don't have an absolute right to enter the plea even in jurisdictions where it is permitted. Some states that permit *nolo contendere* pleas require approval from judges, while other states require approval from judges and prosecutors (Stuckey et al., 2004). Sentencing is the next step for those entering a plea of *nolo contendere.*

Judges set a trial date following a "not guilty" plea. The trial is usually scheduled to occur within two to three weeks following the arraignment (del Carmen, 2004).

Defendants are informed by judges of their rights regarding the forthcoming trial, and a judicial assessment is made concerning the ability of the defendant to stand trial, or an evaluation of the defendant's competency to stand trial is requested. "Not guilty" pleas are more often used in cases involving serious crime (e.g., murder, rape) than in cases involving less serious crimes such as property crimes or drug offenses (Adler et al., 2003).

Federal courts and many state and local jurisdictions abide by the federal provisions offered in the Speedy Trial Act following "not guilty" pleas. Originating in 1974 and amended in 1979 and 1984, the Speedy Trial Act is designed to ensure that defendants are promptly brought to trial as required by the Sixth Amendment right to a speedy trial. Specifically, under the Act, suspects must be charged with an offense within 30 days following their arrest (or the receipt of a summons), and brought to trial in no less than 30 days and no more than 70 days.

PRETRIAL MOTIONS

Prosecutors and defense attorneys ask the court to grant particular requests through various pretrial motions. Although pretrial motions are entered at any time between a not guilty plea and the start of a trial, they are discussed in this chapter as a "not guilty" plea formally signifies the defendant's decision to go to trial, which often instigates the need for motions. Judges consider arguments in the form of written motions (often called petitions), brief arguments, and/or oral arguments from participating attorneys. Separate hearings involving the presentation of evidence are sometimes held in response to pretrial motions. There are many standard, or common, motions, although attorneys can offer unique motions to respond to particular situations that may arise with regard to their case (Ferdico, 1996). Most motions are offered by the defense since the defense is affected by more rights than the prosecution (Stuckey et al., 2004). The major pretrial motions include:

Motion to dismiss. Typically filed by the defense, a motion to dismiss argues that the case should be dismissed and the defendant released. Reasons supporting a motion to dismiss include insufficient evidence, due process violations, and a lack of jurisdiction. Judges can grant two types of dismissals: with prejudice, in which case the defendant cannot be recharged with the same crime; and without prejudice, which essentially means that the case will not proceed to trial, although the prosecutor is permitted to correct the problematic issue and refile charges (Fagin, 2003).

Motion to determine the competency of the accused to stand trial. This motion is designed to protect mentally ill persons from being held responsible for criminal acts. It is a claim that the mental stability of the defendant be examined to determine their ability to stand trial.

Motion to suppress evidence obtained through an unlawful search or seizure. This commonly offered motion argues that particular evidence should be suppressed because it was gathered in violation of the Fourth Amendment.

Motion to suppress confessions, admissions, or other statements made to the police. Similar to the motion to suppress evidence obtained through violations of the Fourth Amendment, this motion seeks to suppress statements made to law enforcement that may be in violation of the *Miranda* rule.

Motion to require the prosecution to disclose the identity of a confidential informant. This motion argues for the prosecution to identify a source of its information, despite the informant being granted confidentiality. Often used in drug cases, this motion is typically denied unless the informant was actively involved in the offense under review (Shelden & Brown, 2003).

Motion for change of venue. Criminal cases are typically held in the jurisdiction in which the offense occurred. Occasionally, however, extensive pretrial publicity may entice either the prosecutor or defense attorney (or both) to suggest the case be relocated to an area with less media scrutiny.

Motion for a continuance. Prosecutors or defense attorneys may, for a variety of reasons, request a continuance or postponement of the case. Continuances are requested due to the need for additional time to prepare a case, illness, difficulty in locating witnesses, and other reasons. Prosecutors remain bound by the Speedy Trial Act even if granted a continuance.

Pretrial motions can be recognized as attorneys jockeying for position for a forthcoming trial, with the shared goal of establishing a fair (or favorable?) playing field. Charges are sometimes dropped and cases dismissed if particular motions are granted. Barkan and Bryjak (2004) suggest motions are 10 times more likely filed in felony cases (10% of cases) than misdemeanor cases (1% of cases). Shelden and Brown (2003, p. 232) note that, for various reasons, motions for continuances and motions to suppress illegally seized evidence are "two of the most common and most important pretrial defense motions" The *motion for discovery*, designed to help defendants better understand the charges against them, is also an option for attorneys and one of the more influential pretrial motions.

DISCOVERY

Discovery, the pretrial procedure in which the prosecution and defense learn more about each other's case, can begin at the arraignment and occur any time up until the trial. It is "the disclosure of deeds, facts, documents, and other material that may be necessary to present an adequate defense or aggressive prosecution" (Barkan & Bryjak, 2004, p. 301), which explains its significance in criminal case processing. A primary purpose served by discovery is to prevent one side from introducing a surprise witness, or other evidence that takes the opposition by surprise and leaves them in a position in which they are unable to adequately react.

Neubauer (2005) notes that "The type of information that is discoverable varies considerably from state to state" (p. 263), ranging from jurisdictions that require limited discovery, in which the prosecution is required to share information regarding confessions and other physical evidence, to jurisdictions with more liberal discovery requirements. Only a few states require prosecutors to disclose almost all of their evidence (Neubauer, 2005).

Pretrial discovery is exercised in two ways: (1) defense attorneys making oral requests to prosecutors for permission to view the material involved in the case; and (2) defense attorneys making written requests in the form of a motion seeking permission to view the prosecution's evidence (Stuckey et al., 2004). Ferdico (1996, p. 56) notes "the state of the law governing discovery is constantly changing, but the trend appears to be in favor of broadening the right of discovery for both the defense and the prosecution."

The prosecution has several disclosure requirements to follow with regard to discovery: On request they must provide the defense with any statements made by the defendant; they must provide copies of medical records and scientific evaluations prepared for them; many states give the defense the opportunity to view the prosecution's documents and tangible objects that will be used in court; and many states require the prosecution to provide the defense with a list of the names and addresses of witnesses who will testify and any testimony or written statements provided earlier by witnesses. The defense is also entitled to a record of any prior felony convictions of the prosecution's witnesses. Defendants in states without discovery provisions must rely on information provided by the prosecution at the preliminary hearing (if applicable) to assess the nature of the state's case against them.

The prosecution is provided some discovery rights by the federal government and most states, although it has no constitutional right to discovery. These rights tend to be narrower in scope than those provided to the defense, and include the defense informing the prosecution if they seek to use an alibi or insanity defense, or if an expert witness will testify that the defendant lacked the mental capacity to testify. In some states the defense must provide the names and previously recorded testimony of witnesses it plans to introduce; and in some states prosecutorial discovery is contingent on the defense seeking discovery (i.e., if the defense doesn't seek discovery, the prosecution is not entitled to it) (Barkan & Bryjak, 2004).

WRAP-UP

The arraignment can be considered a transitional stage in criminal case processing as defendants proceed in two significantly different directions based on their "guilty" or "not guilty" plea. In our case study, James entered a plea of "not guilty," indicating his refusal to plea bargain (although a plea bargain may still occur) and his wish to go to trial. James's attorney felt they had a strong case and plea bargaining would be unfair to his client. The belief that they had a strong case was supported following the successful motion for discovery, through which James's attorney found that the prosecution had some strong evidence, although not what seemed to be enough for a conviction. The judge's refusal to permit a change of venue for the case could hurt James. Pretrial publicity resulting from high levels of crime in the area could provide an obstacle in assembling an unbiased jury. Nevertheless, the case moves forward to trial.

Point–Counterpoint

A few states adopted the "guilty but mentally ill" (GBMI) plea with the intent to ensure that those who commit a crime as a result of a mental illness are cured of their disease and sanctioned for their actions. Other states are considering adopting the plea. *Should offenders who commit their crime while suffering from a mental illness be required to serve time in a mental institution, followed by a sanction?*

Yes: The "guilty but mentally ill" plea should be available in all jurisdictions simply because defendants, regardless of their mental competency, should be held accountable for their actions. The GBMI plea serves two purposes: rehabilitation and punishment. Offenders receive treatment, yet avoid responsibility for their actions in the "not guilty by reason of insanity" plea. The GBMI plea provides some sense of justice for victims and their families as offenders face some form of punishment. It also provides greater accountability for offenders and enhances official monitoring of their behavior, simply because we cannot be sure that the cure for the illness will have a long-lasting effect. In the public's view, the GBMI plea provides greater credibility to the criminal justice system.

No: Violations of criminal law require free choice. Decades of litigation have established that some defendants with mental illness lack the ability to understand their actions. In turn, they cannot, according to criminal law, be guilty. The GBMI is counter to a principle of criminal law. The GBMI plea results in the individual being sanctioned twice for their actions. If they are detained in a mental institution until they are cured, why burden the already overloaded criminal justice system with individuals who have corrected their problem? Are we questioning the ability of psychologists and other professionals to accurately assess who is unfit for society? Research notes that the GBMI verdict has created confusion among jurors and other court professionals, had minimal and unsuccessful results, and generally creates more problems than it solves (Palmer & Hazelrigg, 2000). Perhaps a more effective approach would be to focus on mental health court systems designed to specifically handle cases involving mental illness.

SUGGESTED READING

Adams, J. A., & Blinka, D. D. (2003). *Pretrial motions in criminal prosecutions* (3rd ed.). Charlottesville, VA: LEXISNexus.

Arrigo, B. A. (1996). The behavior of law and psychiatry: Rethinking knowledge construction and the guilty-but-mentally-ill verdict. *Criminal Justice and Behavior, 23*(4), pp. 572–592.

Brennan, W. (1963). The criminal prosecution: Sporting event or quest for truth? *Washington University Law Quarterly*, pp. 279–294.

del Carmen, R. (2004). *Criminal procedure: Law and practice* (6th ed.). Belmont, CA: Wadsworth.

McGinley, H., & Pasewark, R. A. (1989). National survey of the frequency and success of the insanity plea and alternative pleas. *Journal of Psychiatry and Law, 17,* pp. 205–221.

CRITICAL THINKING EXERCISES

1. Consider ways in which you believe pretrial procedures could be more effective and more efficient. Based on these considerations, redesign the pretrial stages with concern for the need to balance crime control and individuals' rights.

2. Identify and discuss several reasons why a greater level of discovery should be extended to the defense. Do you feel the defense is disadvantaged with regard to trial preparation and deserves greater opportunity to examine the prosecution's evidence?

3. Discuss why you believe defendants should or should not be permitted to enter a *nolo contendere* plea.

SHORT ESSAY QUESTIONS

1. What is the purpose of an arraignment? What is the role of the judge at this stage of criminal case processing?

2. Discuss the five pretrial motions you feel have the most significant impact in determining whether or not a defendant will be found guilty.

3. What types of pleas are available for defendants to enter? Are there differences among jurisdictions regarding available pleas?

4. What is discovery and why is it used in the criminal justice system?

5. Why would a defendant enter a *nolo contendere* plea instead of a "guilty" plea?

SECTION III

TRIALS, SENTENCING, AND APPEALS

8 TRIALS

James's case went to trial roughly two weeks after he was arraigned. James went to trial confident he would be acquitted; however, the jury seemed overwhelmed by Jane's testimony and other evidence provided by the prosecution, including testimony from Cedric (the eyewitness) and officials from the crime lab. James and his attorney believed they had a strong case given the lack of direct evidence identifying James's role in the attack. In other words, the prosecution was relying heavily on circumstantial evidence. After deliberating a short while, the jury returned a guilty verdict and James was convicted on one charge of armed robbery. The judge then set a date for a sentencing hearing.

The term *courts* often conjures images of grandiose trials with suspenseful conclusions; however, most trials are rather ordinary in nature. Trials play a significant role in some case processing, although, as noted, most defendants plead guilty following a period of informal plea negotiations with the prosecution. Recent research suggests 95% of felony convictions result from plea agreements (Durose & Langan, 2004; Rainville & Reaves, 2003). Regardless, trials are symbolic of, and associated with recognizing the individual rights of the accused.

At trial, prosecutors and defense attorneys balance concerns for justice and equity with the need to present an effective case. It is argued that trials have degenerated into more of a competition to assure convictions or acquittals than a forum in which to seek justice. Quindlen (2002, p. 64) notes: "Many trials are only tangentially about such sterling-silver notions as the pursuit of justice. Day to day they are more often exercises in gamesmanship, strategy and semantics."

Trials signify the conclusion of pretrial activities and the "beginning of the end" of the defendant's involvement in the court system, although any subsequent appeals may result in the defendant's case returning to court. Defendants will be convicted or acquitted at most trials, and some will result in a hung jury. A conviction results in the case going to sentencing. An acquittal results in the defendant being released from the system. Recent research on felony case processing in the courts of large urban counties suggests that of the small percentage of cases going to trial, most (57%) involved a bench trial (in which judges replace juries and provide a verdict), with 43% involving a jury trial. Roughly 78% of the trials resulted in a conviction, with defendants more likely to be convicted from a bench trial (81%) instead of a jury trial (74%; Rainville & Reaves, 2003).

The defendant, at trial and throughout pretrial procedures, is presumed innocent. At trial the State has the burden of proof to demonstrate that the defendant is guilty beyond a reasonable doubt. One must bear in mind that defendants, at trial, are not found "innocent." It may be possible, for instance, that the defendant is indeed guilty, but the State failed to prove guilt beyond a reasonable doubt.

Bench trials occur in cases in which the defendant either waives their right to a jury trial, or is charged with a petty offense and a jury trial is not permitted. Champion (1998) identifies the advantages and disadvantages of a bench trial. Among the benefits are the expedition of case processing, cases being assessed on merit as opposed to emotion, judges being less likely than juries to consider extralegal factors such as the defendant's appearance, judges being less likely than juries to be influenced by the media, and bench trials being less expensive than jury trials. The disadvantages include judges possibly imposing more severe penalties than juries when considering particular offenses (e.g., drug offenses) and the greater likelihood of corruption in cases where judges act alone.

Jury trials can be deconstructed into seven steps: jury selection, opening statements, presentation of evidence, closing arguments, judge's charge to the jury, jury deliberations, and announcement of a verdict. While these steps make the trial process seem pretty straightforward, various intangibles at each step, such as strategy, justice, and procedural law, intermix. Examining the individual steps in a criminal trial helps us understand the complexities involved in finding justice.

JURY SELECTION

The Sixth Amendment entitles particular defendants to a trial by a public, impartial jury of their peers. Assembling such a jury requires time, effort, and careful consideration of potential jurors. Potential jurors are identified from a variety of sources, including voter registration lists, motor vehicle registration lists, unemployment and welfare roles, water service customer lists, and information from taxes. The group of potential jurors, or *venire*, should represent a cross-section of the community, although impaneling such a jury is not always easy. Not all defendants are entitled to a trial by jury, for instance, juvenile offenders do not maintain the right to have their case heard by a jury, and adult offenders charged with petty offenses are not entitled to a jury trial as the Sixth Amendment encompasses only defendants charged with serious crimes. Some state constitutions, however, do permit a jury trial for anyone charged with a crime for which the penalty could be incarceration (Stuckey et al., 2004).

States vary according to the required size of a jury; however, all states require 12 member juries in capital offense cases, and only a handful allow juries of less than 12 members in felony cases. Some states permit misdemeanor trials with only six jurors, while others permit criminal trials with seven or eight jurors. Alternate jurors sit through the trial and are present during jury deliberations. They do not, however, actively participate in jury deliberations unless a member of the jury is dismissed and a replacement is needed.

Prosecutors and defense attorneys use different *challenges* in attempts to impanel an appropriate jury. A *challenge to the array* is typically offered by defense attorneys who feel a jury pool is not representative of the community or is biased in some manner. This challenge takes place prior to jury selection (Schmalleger, 2005). Actual jury selection involves the prosecution and defense attorney questioning potential jurors in a process called *voir dire*, and using challenges to eliminate those whom they believe would be unfit for a jury. Attorney and judicial questioning during *voir dire* assists in their attempts to construct a bias-free jury with no preconceived notions of guilt or innocence. Trial judges in the federal courts conduct the questioning during *voir dire*, although judges may permit attorneys to conduct the questioning or provide questions for the judge to ask. Attorneys conduct the questioning in most state courts (del Carmen, 2004).

If, during questioning, attorneys identify a particular reason why a potential juror may be unsuitable for the trial, they issue a *challenge for cause*, in which case the juror would be dismissed should the court recognize the attorney's claim. *Peremptory challenges* are another type of challenge available to attorneys. Peremptory challenges are offered by an attorney, again during *voir dire*, who does not wish to have a potential juror impaneled, although the attorney is not required to offer a reason or justification for the dismissal. Attorneys are limited in the number of peremptory challenges they can use, and states vary in the number of peremptory challenges they permit. The number of peremptory challenges may depend on the seriousness of the charge, with more challenges available in cases involving more serious offenses (del Carmen,

2004). Unless a challenge for cause can be offered, attorneys must accept all jurors once they've used all of the peremptory challenges.

Not everyone is permitted to serve on a jury. Ex-felons, individuals below a particular age, nonresidents of the United States, those unable to speak English, and individuals with a connection to the criminal justice system (e.g., police officers, judges, etc.) or with personal connections to the case are disqualified from jury duty (Shelden & Brown, 2003). Jurors are paid anywhere from a few dollars up to $40 per day and most serve a short period of time.

Once a jury is selected and alternates are identified, the judge determines whether the jury should be sequestered, or isolated from the public, during the course of the trial. Although sequestering a jury is an option, most jurors in cases lasting more than one day are permitted to go home in the evenings; however, they may not discuss the case with anyone. Sequestering a jury is often done out of concern for publicity surrounding the trial and to prevent jury tampering.

OPENING STATEMENTS

Although they are not required to do so, attorneys may begin the trial with an opening statement to the jury. The prosecution typically provides the first opening statement and is followed by the defense attorney. Opening statements are less effective and less often used in bench trials as judges, who are typically privy to numerous trials, do not require the benefits of opening statements (Senna & Siegel, 2002). Among other things, opening statements are designed to "make it easier for jurors to grasp the meaning and significance of evidence and testimony and to keep them from becoming confused by the complexities of the case" (Territo et al., 2004, p. 374). The opening statement provides juries with an overview of each side's case. Some judges permit attorneys to speak at length during opening statements, while other judges impose a time limit (Barkan & Bryjak, 2004).

"Opinions, conclusions, references to the character of the accused, argumentative statements, and references to matters on which evidence will not be offered are out of place" during the opening statements, and attorneys may object to them (del Carmen, 2004, p. 47). Attorneys identify the evidence they intend to introduce at trial during opening statements, although no evidence is formally introduced. Attorneys work under a "good faith" requirement that the content of their opening statement will include only the information they believe will be permitted during trial. In other words, evidence they, in good faith, believe will be excluded during trial should not be part of the opening statement. Trial judges assess whether a statement is permissible.

The opening statement assists the jury in understanding forthcoming events in the trial. Such information can be especially helpful in trials expected to last an extended period of time. The opening statement can be described as "a kind of 'road map' that describes the destination that each attorney hopes to reach and outlines how she or he plans to reach it" (Gaines & Miller, 2003, p. 339). It provides each attorney the opportunity to introduce their case and confront the jury. This opportunity for introduction is significant in that, as the saying goes, "you can never make a second first impression." Opening statements have a notable impact on jury decision making, as jurors tend to side with attorneys who provide the most powerful opening statement (Pyszczynski & Wrightsman, 1981).

Strategically, some defense attorneys choose not to offer an opening statement, or provide a brief opening statement, with the intent to better understand the nature of the prosecution's case. If the defense chooses to offer a traditional opening statement, they would be restricted to abide by the claims offered in the statement, otherwise they risk confusing the jury. By not offering an opening statement, or offering a brief statement, the defense leaves flexibility in the direction and nature of its defense.

PRESENTATION OF EVIDENCE

The State is the first to present evidence to the jury following opening statements. Evidence presented at trial is bound by the rules of evidence, which, among other things, state that evidence must be *competent*, or legally permissible; *material*, or having a direct bearing on the case; and *relevant*, or applicable to the case. Three types of evidence may be introduced at trial: circumstantial evidence, direct evidence, and real evidence. Circumstantial, or indirect, evidence does not directly link the defendant and the crime, and can be interpreted in multiple ways. It is concerned with possibilities and probabilities, leaving the jury to determine whether particular circumstances are favorable or unfavorable, or indicting or nonindicting, to the defendant. Direct evidence is any evidence that provides a direct link between the defendant and the crime (e.g., eyewitness testimony). Real evidence is physical evidence, which can be circumstantial or direct. Fingerprints, notes, and weapons are examples of real evidence.

While it would seem that direct and real evidence would more heavily influence a jury than circumstantial evidence, the significance of circumstantial evidence should not be overlooked. For instance, the recent, high-profile conviction of Scott Peterson on charges of murdering his wife and their unborn son was largely based on circumstantial evidence; the case involved little physical evidence.

Questioning begins with the prosecution's direct examination of their witnesses. Following the prosecution's questioning of each witness, the defense questions the prosecution's witness in cross-examination. After cross-examination the prosecution has the opportunity to ask witnesses additional questions in light of the cross-examination in what is called "redirect examination." Following redirect examination, the defense is again given the opportunity to question witnesses in "recross-examination." The defense attorney is not required at any point to question the prosecution's witnesses. The prosecution has no opportunity to ask additional questions of a witness should the defense choose not to redirect or recross. The prosecution rests when it has presented all of its evidence and witnesses. The defense then presents its case. Objections to questions asked and responses given are offered by both the prosecution and defense during the presentation of evidence. The judge either sustains (permits them) or overrules (denies) them.

The defense customarily requests a motion for a directed verdict following the prosecution's presentation of evidence. This motion argues that the prosecution has not presented a strong enough case to go forward, thus the charges should be dropped prior to the defense presenting its case. This motion is rarely granted (Fagin, 2003). The procedures for introducing and examining the defense's evidence are the same for the prosecution, although the defense is not required to present a case, and would choose not to offer evidence should they feel the prosecution has not proven guilt beyond a reasonable doubt. The attorneys are finished introducing new evidence once the defense rests. They can, however, attempt to refute evidence already presented.

Following the defense's case, the prosecution can introduce witness testimony to refute testimony given from a defense witness in what is known as rebuttal. This testimony may be followed by testimony from the defense, discrediting testimony offered during rebuttal, in what is known as surrebuttal. Few trials proceed through all of the aforementioned steps involved in the presentation of evidence (Fagin, 2003).

One of the major decisions made by defense attorneys during a trial concerns whether or not to put the defendant on the stand. Juries are likely interested in hearing from the defendant, yet the defense may find it harmful to permit the defendant to testify. Defendants may use their Fifth Amendment protection from self-incrimination and refuse to testify.

Defendants enter either an alibi or affirmative defense. An alibi defense suggests the defendant, who assumes no responsibility for the crime, could not have committed the crime as they were somewhere else at the time. Affirmative defenses, on the other hand, are offered when defendants are willing to admit to committing the behavior in question, although they do not admit guilt. Affirmative defenses are used when the defense does not challenge that the defendant committed the act, however, the defense does challenge legal responsibility for the actions. Self-defense, infancy, insanity, duress, coercion, and entrapment are among the affirmative defenses. Affirmative defenses can pose difficulties for the defense as they require demonstration. In other words, prior to entering an affirmative defense the onus was on the prosecution to prove the defendant's guilt beyond a reasonable doubt; the defense was not required to prove anything. Affirmative defenses, however, require the defense to prove that the defendant is not legally responsible for the act.

CLOSING ARGUMENTS

Closing arguments follow the presentation of the evidence and are "often the most dramatic parts of the trial" (Neubauer, 2005, p. 323). They enable attorneys to summarize their cases and explain to the jury why their case is stronger than the opposition's. References are made to exhibits, evidence, testimony, and other items presented in the trial. States vary regarding the order in which closing arguments are offered, however, the prosecution typically presents closing arguments prior to the defense, and has the option of rebuttal, or having the final say. This format seemingly favors the prosecution, although the prosecution has the burden of proving guilt beyond a reasonable doubt. Some jurisdictions permit the defense to go first, followed by the prosecution.

Closing arguments enable attorneys to "tie up" any loose ends, for instance, explaining why a defendant didn't take the stand. However, attorneys are prevented from entering personal opinions or new evidence. Instead, attorneys summarize the evidence that was presented at trial in an attempt to persuade the jury to support their respective arguments. Closing arguments, or summation, typically involve the prosecution encouraging the jury to recognize the State's case as strong enough to find the defendant guilty beyond a reasonable doubt, and the defense highlighting the shortcomings of the prosecution's case or demonstrating the defendant's lack of culpability. Despite the drama often associated with closing arguments, attorneys must be wary of becoming too emotional during this phase. In the interests of the law, cases should be weighed by juries on their merit, not the emotional persuasion of a skilled attorney.

JUDGE'S CHARGE TO THE JURY

Judges are required to offer instructions to the jury following closing arguments. The judge prepares the *charge to the jury,* which is "a written document explaining how the law is applicable to the case" (Fagin, 2003, p. 328). These charges are usually prepared in an informal charging conference involving the judge and trial attorneys (Gaines & Miller, 2003). Among the items included in the charge to the jury are a reminder to remain impartial; a statement noting the crime for which the defendant is accused; definitions of legal concepts pertinent to the case; a reminder that the prosecution has the burden of proving guilt beyond a reasonable doubt; and procedural instructions, for instance, directions for contacting the judge should they need to do so (Adler et al., 2003). The judge, through jury instructions, also explains what evidence may or may not be considered in finding a verdict. Finally, the judge provides a list of potential verdicts for the jury to consider.

The judge's instructions to the jury may be lengthy and are subject to appellate review. One must keep in mind that juries are not particularly familiar with the law, thus the directions can be the most influential component of a trial. Some scholars question the effectiveness of jury instructions, particularly regarding whether juries always understand the instructions (e.g., Dattu, 1998; Foglia, 2003) and whether the instructions have any impact on how well-equipped juries are to render a decision (e.g., Steele & Thornburg, 1991). Dattu (1998) suggests the use of illustrated jury instructions to assist jurors who may find difficulty grasping written jury instructions.

JURY DELIBERATIONS AND VERDICT

Juries elect a foreperson, or one is selected, prior to beginning formal deliberations. The foreperson has the responsibility of presiding over the deliberations and reading the verdict in the courtroom. Jurors are permitted to examine evidence introduced at trial and may request portions of the transcript during deliberations.

The secrecy of jury deliberations makes it difficult to fully understand what occurs during this stage of adjudication. What is known about jury deliberations stems from studies of mock juries and interviews of jurors following their dismissal. We can also understand a bit more about jury deliberations based on the questions jurors ask judges during deliberations. Jurors, who are often prevented from taking notes during trial, sit passively, sometimes anxiously, during the trial prior to deliberations. The length of deliberations may be short, for instance, when there is overwhelming or sparse evidence. In contrast, deliberations may take days or sometimes weeks.

The Supreme Court ruled that unanimity is not necessary in noncapital cases although most jurisdictions require a unanimous decision. Federal cases, which require 12-member juries, must be unanimous. Judges will sometimes issue an Allen Charge to juries unable to reach agreement. In these cases judges recharge the jury with a new set of instructions designed to encourage agreement, and suggest to dissenting jurors that their objections may not be appropriate given the rest of the group's consensus. Finding agreement among a group of citizens gathered from all walks of society, with varied interpretations of the case and instructions, and differing levels of attentiveness during the trial can pose problems. Schmalleger (2005, p. 441) notes that "In highly charged cases, emotions are often difficult to separate from fact, and during deliberations, some juries are dominated by one or two members with forceful personalities." He adds that juror deliberations are sometimes affected by fear of retaliation in response to their decision.

Following the announcement of a verdict in the courtroom, jurors may be polled by the trial attorneys. The polling enables the attorneys to ensure that all (or the necessary number) of jurors agree with the verdict. Champion (1998, p. 252) suggests that "It is unlikely that a particular juror will tell the judge that he or she did not agree with the jury's decision." The jury may be sent back for further deliberations should an insufficient number agree with the verdict, or the judge may rule the case a mistrial, which would result in the need for a new trial with different jurors. It is also possible for the case to be dismissed should an insufficient number of jurors agree with the verdict. Fagin (2003) notes that only about 6% of cases result in a jury being unable to come to a verdict. There is no limit to how many times a case may be retried. A hung jury may be reason for a prosecutor not to retry the case.

Alternative approaches are offered to improve the trial process. Among the alternatives are having citizen-based juries replaced with a panel of judges who would offer verdicts and sentences. Some propose the use of professional jurors, who would be paid employees knowledgeable of the law and familiar with the court process. Among the benefits of professional juries are dependability, knowledge, and equity (Schmalleger, 2005). Furthermore, an increasing number of courts are permitting jury members to take notes during trial and more actively participate in trials by asking questions to witnesses. Some jurors in California are presented with notebooks containing trial exhibits and legal papers to facilitate deliberations (Willing, 2005). Some courts in Maryland provide jurors legal instructions prior to trial (as opposed to after the sides present their cases) as a legal roadmap to help them more effectively evaluate testimony. There are, of course, limitations to each of these approaches, for instance, defense attorneys argue that permitting jurors to ask questions during trial enables prosecutors to possibly alter their case, as juror questions may provide a preview of how jurors view the case (Willing, 2005).

WRAP-UP

James's case was heard by a jury, and, like many other felony trial cases, resulted in a guilty verdict. Part of the reason behind the large number of convictions at trial is the thorough examination of the case to this point and plea bargaining. Prosecutors are generally less willing to plea bargain cases they believe they can win at trial. James now moves forward to the sentencing phase of criminal case processing, as he anxiously awaits to hear his fate. He will appeal the case, as the trial judge did not permit the introduction of a crucial piece of evidence, which would have strengthened James's case.

In many ways the adjudication process can be compared to a boxing match. The opponents prepare for battle (e.g., boxers through physical training, attorneys through evidence collection and case building), and stage an event in search of a particular outcome (e.g., boxers wish to win the match; attorneys hope to find justice. . . and win the case). The judge in a criminal trial is akin to a boxing referee, ruling on what is and what is not permitted. In fact, one of the most famous boxing referees, Mills Lane, was also a judge. The jury observes the happenings and generally has the final say, similar to the role played by boxing judges. While the adjudication process lacks the violence of a boxing match, it certainly can contain as much drama.

Point–Counterpoint

Some question the presence of video cameras in the courtroom. The Sixth Amendment guarantees the right to a public trial, although there is concern that cameras could affect courtroom proceedings. *Should cameras be permitted in the courtroom?*

Yes: Video cameras in the courtroom provide several benefits, including the increased public awareness of our judicial system. To be honest, few people understand precisely how things occur in our court systems. Cameras would help provide an accurate record of events in the courtroom and likely deter some judicial or attorney misconduct. Furthermore, the public has a right to know what happens in our courts, and judges maintain the right to remove the cameras should they appear to influence court proceedings. Some evidence suggests that cameras do influence the courtroom personnel's behavior, although other research suggests it has no impact.

Common sense would suggest that cameras impact participants to behave in a more professional manner. Perhaps the most important question surrounding video cameras in the courtroom is: "What's to hide?" The public has a right to know what goes on in our courts.

No: Allowing video cameras into our courtrooms would turn our courts into a forum for reality television. Citizens would lose respect for the institution, as court proceedings would become an avenue of entertainment as opposed to a setting for justice (e.g., the O.J. Simpson trial). Cameras can affect jurors, who may be intimidated by their exposure, and attorneys and judges have been known to alter their behavior when being filmed. The Sixth Amendment provides defendants the right to a public trial, although that *protection* addressed the harms associated with secret hearings. In particular, the Sixth Amendment was designed to protect defendants, not make them the assumed villains of reality television.

SUGGESTED READING

Burnett, D. G. (2001, August 26). Anatomy of a verdict: The view from a juror's chair. *New York Times Magazine*, pp. 32–37.

Foglia, W. D. (2003). They know not what they do: Unguided and misguided discretion in Pennsylvania capital cases. *Justice Quarterly, 20*(1), pp. 187–211.

Miller, D. W. (2001, November 23). Jury consulting on trial: Scholars doubt claims that jurors' votes can be predicted. *Chronicle of Higher Education*, pp. A15–A16.

Rao, P. A. (1999). Keeping the science court out of the jurybox: Helping the jury manage scientific evidence. *Social Epistemology, 13*(2), pp. 129–145.

Rose, M. R. (1999). The peremptory challenge accused of race or gender discrimination? Some data from one county. *Law and Human Behavior, 23*(6), pp. 695–702.

CRITICAL THINKING EXERCISES

1. Identify five strengths and five weaknesses of trials. Briefly discuss what can be done to address the weaknesses.

2. Do you believe jury selection is fair? What are the limitations of current jury selection practices?

3. Do you feel the prosecution has an unfair advantage during the trial? If so, explain how. If not, explain why.

SHORT ESSAY QUESTIONS

1. Identify and briefly discuss the ordering of the steps involved in a jury trial.

2. How are juries selected?

3. What is included in the judge's charge to the jury? In other words, what instructions are typically provided to the jury?

4. Explain the *voir dire* process. What are the differences between challenges for cause and peremptory challenges?

5. What types of defenses are available to defendants?

9 SENTENCING

James was convicted of armed robbery and sentenced to 6 years in state prison. He and his attorney disagreed with the severity of the penalty; however, the judge mentioned that this particular sentence was given in light of the seriousness of the current offense and with consideration of James's previous criminal record consisting of four misdemeanor convictions and two felony arrests. In announcing the sentence the judge stated that he "hopes this penalty will cause James to reflect on his actions and assume a different lifestyle upon his release." James's attorney will file an appeal citing judicial misconduct in the trial. Meanwhile, James was escorted out of the courtroom and taken to state prison where he will begin his sentence. With time off for good behavior, James expects to be released from prison in about 3 years.

Criminal sentencing is one of the most controversial aspects of criminal case processing. For instance, a judge may believe a particular sentence is fair, yet others may see the penalty as too harsh or perhaps too lenient. Or, a judge may be required to impose a particular sentence designated by law, even though all in the courtroom disagree with the appropriateness of the sanction. The power to sanction an individual is like few other powers provided professionals in any field, and the vague protections offered by the U.S. Constitution result in great discretion when imposing criminal sentences. In turn, sanctioning bodies, including legislators, judges, and juries, are expected to act in accordance with the ideals of our systems of justice.

Sentences are decided solely by a judge in most states, although under certain sentencing structures (e.g., mandatory sentences) sentences are statutorily defined. A few states provide defendants the choice of being sentenced by the judge or jury following a jury trial. Judges may offer a sentence immediately after a guilty plea or guilty verdict in less serious cases, or cases in which the penalty is statutorily prescribed. Some states and the federal government follow sentencing guidelines with the intent to provide greater consistency in sentencing decisions; other states provide greater judicial discretion in sentencing decisions. States that permit juries to determine sentences proceed in one of two ways: requiring juries to offer a sentence immediately following a guilty verdict or offering a sentence after the rules of evidence are relaxed and the prosecution and defense disclose information, including material that may not have been permitted at trial (e.g., the offender's prior record).

Imposing a sentence typically does not immediately follow a guilty verdict in cases involving a serious crime, simply because many states require the preparation of a presentence investigation report (PSIR) to assist with sentence decision making. The PSIR, which is either required by law or requested by a judge, is typically prepared by a probation or parole officer who, in addition to providing background information regarding the convicted, offers a recommendation as to what they believe is an appropriate sentence. The PSIR offers only a sentence recommendation; judges are permitted to disregard the suggestion and impose the sentence they see appropriate. Sentences are imposed by a judge in plea-bargained cases, although judges typically follow the agreed-upon sentence generated through plea negotiations.

In many instances judges are permitted to suspend the sentence in lieu of probation or some other form of community supervision for a particular period of time. Suspects who violate the conditions of their agreement are typically required to serve their original, suspended sentence.

FACTORS INFLUENCING SENTENCING DECISIONS

Among the individuals influencing sentencing decisions are victims, who in some jurisdictions offer victim impact statements. These statements include their views on the incident and what they believe is an appropriate penalty. Legislators also influence sentencing decisions through supporting more or less punitive sentencing structures. Probation and parole officers who prepare presentence investigation reports also influence criminal sentences. Furthermore, offenders undoubtedly influence sentencing decisions, as do defense attorneys and prosecutors. Attorneys for both sides offer input regarding what they believe is an appropriate sentence at the sentencing hearing. Judges consider this input, and possibly information from the presentence investigator, who may be called to testify as to how they collected information on the offender and generated their sentence recommendation.

Needless to say, sentencing decisions are influenced by a variety of individuals and variables. Sentencing bodies must consider aggravating (factors that would enhance a penalty) and mitigating (factors that would reduce a penalty) variables in their decision. In addition to this information, a variety of factors are considered in sentencing decisions, including the seriousness of the offense; the offender's criminal history; whether or not the crime involved violence; and whether or not money was the motivation for the offense (Senna & Siegel, 2002). Extralegal variables such as race, age, gender, socioeconomic status, and victim characteristics may also influence sentencing decisions.

PURPOSES OF CRIMINAL SANCTIONS

What do we hope to accomplish when we sanction offenders? Why do we make some individuals pick up trash on the highway? Why do we place some individuals in prison, and why do we sometimes execute people? Understanding the purposes of criminal sentencing helps answer these and related questions. Sentences are sometimes imposed with the intent to rehabilitate individuals. The goal of *rehabilitation* begins with attempts to understand why the crime occurred and help offenders abstain from future criminal behavior. In other words, it is believed that the crime occurred because of a reparable shortcoming in the individual.

Sentences are sometimes offered with the goal of *incapacitation.* Incapacitation as a goal of criminal sentencing involves physically preventing one from committing further harm to society. The belief is that offenders who are detained in prison or jail cannot physically harm the larger society. Incapacitation exists in forms other than incarceration, for instance, chemical castration is seen by some as appropriate for those convicted of sex crimes. Recent efforts involving selective incapacitation, or identifying and incarcerating dangerous offenders, have been met with some controversy (e.g., Visher, 1987).

Retribution, or "an eye for an eye," is also a goal of criminal sentencing. Retribution is payback for criminal behavior. Criminal sentences with the goal of retribution are assessed on whether or not they provide the offender with punishment as painful as the harm they inflicted. Retribution aims to directly associate punishment with the criminal event and is a principle consideration in most criminal sentences. Punishment remains popular in criminal sentencing, although some argue that "two wrongs don't make a right."

Some sentences include *deterrence* as a goal. These sentences seek to discourage individuals from committing further crime, for instance, through the use or threat of lengthy prison sentences. Specific or special deterrence involves sanctions designed to deter particular individuals, while general deterrence seeks to discourage a general audience from engaging in particular behavior. Deterrence is based on the belief that individuals make rational choices in deciding to commit crime, thus, it is felt that "unpleasant" sentences discourage future criminal behavior.

Restoration is another goal of criminal sentences. Restoration as a goal generally involves attempts to restore the victim and offender to their places in society. The belief is that in some instances offenders, and society in general, would benefit from reintegrating offenders, as opposed to traditional practices of outcasting them. Restoration is based, in part, on the belief that human lives are not things to be discarded simply due to illegal behavior. Perhaps the most important goals of restoration involve repairing the harms done to victims, and restoring them to the lives they had prior to their victimization. Restitution and victim–offender mediation are two of the more common components of restoration.

Criminal sentences often maintain more than one of the above-noted goals. For instance, sentences such as community service (e.g., picking up trash on highways) could serve the purposes of deterrence and retribution. The particular purposes of criminal sanctions are not specifically noted by judges, although one can typically determine what the sentencing body had in mind when imposing a sentence. For example, those sentenced to drug rehabilitation are targeted for rehabilitation. Those sentenced to life in prison without the opportunity for parole are likely targets of incapacitation, retribution, and, perhaps, general deterrence. The judge in James's case hoped that the sentence James received would cause James to reflect on his actions and assume a different lifestyle upon his release. At the most basic level, the judge's *statement* suggests he's hoping for James to be rehabilitated, although the judge's *actions* suggest the focus was on retribution, incapacitation, and deterrence.

TYPES OF SENTENCES

Part of the controversy surrounding criminal sentences stems from both qualitative and quantitative issues. Specifically, sentencing bodies must determine an appropriate sanction (quality) and an appropriate duration for the sentence (quantity). Identifying an appropriate sentence requires careful consideration of a variety of factors and ensuring that opportunities exist for offenders to serve their sentence in particular capacities. For example, a judge may want to sentence a drug offender to a drug treatment facility, only to find no availability in the local rehabilitation facilities. In turn, the judge must find appropriate alternatives.

Offenders may receive probation, which involves offenders serving a period of time in the community under the supervision of a probation officer. Probationers' freedoms are restricted per the terms of their probation agreement, which could require offenders to submit to random drug testing, maintain employment, and restrict their associations with particular individuals, among other provisions. Fines and restitution require offenders to make reparations for their behavior. Fines, the most common form of punishment, are financial sums of money paid to the government. Restitution involves victims receiving money and/or services from the offender in an attempt to make amends for their criminal behavior. Community service is a sanction that requires offenders to perform some form of labor benefiting the community in an attempt to compensate society for their crime. Community service is most often recognized as offenders picking up trash on roadsides, however, it could involve other activities such as offenders tutoring underprivileged children, mowing public lawns, or washing government vehicles. Some offenders are sentenced to substance abuse treatment centers designed to help them overcome difficulties they may have with certain substances. Offenders sentenced to day reporting centers are required to report daily to a central location where they meet with a supervising officer who ensures that the offender is using their time productively (e.g., in a classroom, in therapy, at work, etc.).

Some offenders are sentenced to home confinement with electronic monitoring. These offenders must remain within the confines of their home unless permitted to leave on occasion. One form of electronic monitoring involves the offender wearing a bracelet that transmits an electronic signal to the offender's supervising agent when the offender leaves home. The supervisor then determines if the departure is acceptable (e.g., the offender leaves home on their way to work or counseling). Offenders sentenced to incarceration serve shorter sentences in jails. Longer periods of incarceration (generally a year or more) are served in a state or federal prison.

Capital punishment, or the death penalty, is the most extreme sanction and the most controversial. It is reserved for the most heinous offenses. This list of criminal sanctions is not comprehensive, and sanctions may be combined. For instance, an offender could receive a fine and probation.

SENTENCING STRUCTURES

The statutes of the jurisdiction in which a crime is committed may determine the sentence one receives. Several sentencing structures, or strategic approaches to sentencing, have been implemented in the United States over the past few decades. Among the sentencing structures are indeterminate sentences, determinate sentences, and mandatory sentences. Although in recent years indeterminate sentencing has given way in many jurisdictions to more punitive approaches, "The indeterminate sentence is still the most widely used type of sentence in the United States. Convicted offenders are typically given a 'light' minimum sentence that must be served and a lengthy maximum sentence that is the outer boundary" of how long one might remain incarcerated (Senna & Siegel, 2002, p. 408). The length of time served is to be determined by a judge who sets the parameters, and the correctional agency, which determines when the offender is prepared for reentry to society. Like other sentencing structures, there are variations regarding the actual practice of indeterminate sentence (see, e.g., Senna & Siegel, 2002, p. 408). The premise behind indeterminate sentencing is to individualize penalties with the intent to rehabilitate offenders (Senna & Siegel, 2002).

Some suggest indeterminate sentencing provides too much discretion and is too soft on criminals. In response, some jurisdictions moved toward determinate sentences, which, as originally developed, involve a set period of incarceration up to a maximum time set by statutory law. For instance, the law may permit up to 25 years in prison for armed robbery, however, judges may give a 15-year sentence based on mitigating circumstances. Determinate sentences specify a period of time to be served in prison without the opportunity for parole, although inmates can be released early through accumulating good time credits for good behavior in prison.

Like determinate sentences, mandatory sentences were introduced to contain judicial discretion and become increasingly punitive toward criminals. "Mandatory sentencing laws generally limit the judge's discretionary power to impose any disposition but that authorized by the legislature" (Senna & Siegel, 2002, p. 413). Mandatory sentences are designed to facilitate equal treatment for all, thus eliminating consideration of race, gender, age, and other extralegal variables. Most states have replaced discretionary sentencing with determinate sentencing for particular serious crimes, or for offenders who meet particular criteria. For instance, some states impose enhanced sentences through habitual offender laws or three strikes penalties, which are designed to address repeat offenders.

RECENT RESEARCH

Recent research on felony sentences in 2002 sheds light on the nature of sentencing in state courts. For instance, Durose and Langan (2004) found that state and federal courts sentenced an estimated 1,114,217 offenders, with state courts accounting for

94% of the total. Drug offenders (32.4%) constituted the largest percentage of felons sentenced in state courts, followed by property offenders (30.9%) and violent offenders (18.8%). Convicted felons in state courts were most likely to be sentenced to state prison (41%), followed by straight probation (31%) and jail (28%). Those sentenced to jail received an average sentence of 7 months; those sentenced to prison received an average sentence of about 53 months. The average probation sentence was 38 months.

Durose and Langan (2004) add that the average prison sentence was shorter in 2002 than in 1992 (4.5 years compared to 6 years), although felons in 2002 were serving a longer percentage of their sentences than in 1994 (51% compared to 38%). The median time from arrest to sentencing was roughly 6 months in 2002 and about 78% of convicted felons were sentenced within a year of arrest. Most felons convicted in state court in 2002 were male (83%), white (60%, followed by black, 37%), and ranged in age from 20 to 29 (41%, followed by the 30–39 age group, 29%). The mean age of convicted felons was 32 years old (Durose & Langan, 2004).

WRAP-UP

The controversial practice of criminal sentencing continues to undergo reform and criticism from various groups. A primary obstacle in finding agreement regarding sentencing decisions stems from conflicting views of the underlying purposes of criminal sentences. Some view sentencing as an opportunity to "teach a lesson," while others view sentencing as an opportunity to help those most in need.

As a white male in his mid-twenties, James clearly fits the mold of the typical offender sentenced in state court. His crime and the fact that he went to trial are atypical of criminal case processing in that most crime is minor and most cases are plea bargained. James must now physically and mentally prepare for incarceration. He retains hope as his attorney prepares to file an appeal.

Point–Counterpoint

Judges are sometimes permitted to let victims offer input regarding their views on the sentencing of offenders via victim impact statements. The introduction of victim impact statements, it is argued, focuses attention on the worthiness of the victim instead of the particular harm. *Should victim impact statements be permitted during the sentencing hearing?*

Yes: Victim impact statements should be permitted during the sentencing hearing simply because they give victims a voice in criminal case processing and provide a more thorough perspective on the incident. The opportunity to offer input provides victims an opportunity to address the harm and pain they've suffered, which may help them put the victimization behind them. Victim impact statements also provide those in the courtroom, particularly offenders, an opportunity to understand the pain and suffer-

ing caused by crime. Hearing the input of victims may help offenders understand the consequences of their actions and discourage them from further criminal behavior.

No: Victim impact statements should not be permitted during the sentencing phase for several reasons. First, offenders are to be punished for their actions, regardless of the credibility of the victim. Second, victim impact statements may unfairly bias the sentencing body with statements that may generate a high level of emotions. Third, some victims may wish to find closure with regard to the victimization; however, the grievance process may be prolonged if victims anticipate having to speak at the sentencing hearing. Finally, there is an inherent bias in victim impact statements in that some victims are viewed as more credible than others. For instance, should the murder of a prostitute be treated differently from the murder of a school teacher?

SUGGESTED READING

Bushway, S. D., & Piehl, A. M. (2001). Judging judicial discretion: Legal factors and racial discrimination in sentencing. *Law and Society Review, 35*(4), pp. 733–764.

Crawford, C., Chiricos, T., & Kleck, G. (1998). Race, racial threat, and sentencing of habitual offenders. *Criminology, 36*(3), pp. 481–511.

Engen, R. L., Gainey, R. R., Crutchfield, R. D., & Weis, J. G. (2003). Discretion and disparity under sentencing guidelines: The role of departures and structured sentencing alternatives. *Criminology, 41*(1), pp. 99–130.

Kovandzic, T. V. (2001). The impact of Florida's habitual offender law on crime. *Criminology, 39*(1), pp. 179–203.

Myers, B., & Arbuthnot, J. (1999). The effects of victim impact evidence on the verdicts and sentencing judgments of mock jurors. *Journal of Offender Rehabilitation, 29*(3/4), pp. 95–112.

CRITICAL THINKING EXERCISES

1. Identify the goals of the various criminal sanctions identified in the chapter. For instance, it is noted that rehabilitation is the goal of sentencing one to substance abuse treatment. What are the primary purposes of the other sanctions?

2. A judge sentences a repeat offender to the maximum time permitted by law and upon issuing the sentence tells the offender: "This sentence is designed to teach you a lesson and physically prevent you from committing further crime." Discuss what you believe are the specific goals the judge had in mind when issuing this sentence.

3. Assume you are a judge charged with sentencing a first-time offender convicted of driving under the influence. What sentence would you give this offender? Why?

SHORT ESSAY QUESTIONS

1. Identify and briefly discuss the various criminal sanctions.

2. Who influences criminal sentencing? What extralegal factors are sometimes considered in sentence decision making? Should these variables be considered?

3. Are judges always responsible for handing out criminal sentences? In what circumstances would a jury determine a sentence?

4. What is the purpose of the presentence investigation report? Who prepares the report and what does it contain?

5. What are the purposes of criminal sanctions? Which do you believe are most evident in current sentencing practices?

10 APPEALS

James appealed his case to the state intermediate court of appeals following his conviction. His argument centered around the trial judge's decision to exclude testimony from his friend who claimed to have assisted James with house repairs shortly before the time of the offense for which James was convicted. The trial court judge ruled that the circumstantial evidence was not permissible because he believed James would've been able to commit the crime even if he was with his friend prior to the crime. The appellate judges reviewed the transcript of the trial proceedings, listened to oral arguments from both the prosecution and defense, and upheld the lower court ruling. James then issued a writ of habeas corpus contesting his confinement in state prison. A federal court reviewed the writ and determined that no action was needed with regard to James's case. In other words, James's case was denied on merits.

Criminal courts can be separated into trial and appellate courts. James's case was originally heard in a trial court, yet his appeals were considered in appellate courts. Thirty-nine states have intermediate appellate courts and all states have a court of last resort (often called the state supreme court), which hears all appeals in the 11 states without an intermediate court of appeal. Defendants are entitled to submit their case for review to the U.S. Supreme Court following state appellate review, although the Supreme Court hears very few of the cases they receive.

Defendants have the right to appeal following their conviction and the judge's ruling in all post-trial motions; they also have the right to counsel during the appellate stage. Appellate courts help ensure that a defendant's rights were protected according to the state or federal constitution, criminal court procedural law, and substantive law. Territo and colleagues (2004, p. 417) note that "The right to appeal the guilty verdict in a criminal trial is one of the most important aspects of due process."

APPEALS AND APPELLATE COURTS

Appeals are requests for a higher court to review trial court proceedings. They are discretionary in that the losing party at trial is not obligated to appeal the decision, with the exception of capital punishment cases. The appellate court does not conduct a new trial. Instead, appellate court judges consider brief oral arguments from attorneys and the trial court transcript. The burden of proof is on the appellant to demonstrate why the decision should be reversed or altered. Sentences of death or life in prison are automatically reviewed by the highest court of appeal in most states.

Most lower court decisions are upheld on appeal. Occasionally an appellate court will rule that the lower court erred and the conviction should be overturned and returned for trial at the lower court, with the court addressing the erroneous issue in the initial trial. The appeal is not a retrying of the case, and appellate courts typically are not concerned with factual evidence. Appellate courts hear far fewer cases than trial courts.

Appellate courts primarily address the legal issues involved at trial, leaving assessment of factual issues to judges and/or juries (Ferdico, 1996). Appellate courts review concerns surrounding the introduction of illegally seized evidence, improper jury instructions, and denial of counsel or a fair trial. The written opinions offered by appellate court judges become part of the law and may be used in future cases involving similar issues. This practice of policy formulation through written opinions is one of the primary functions of appellate courts (Neubauer, 2005). Through reviewing trial court decisions, appellate courts promote consistency among trial courts and discourage judicial misconduct.

The *contemporaneous objection* rule states that the appealing party "must preserve its claim by making a specific timely objection at or before trial," otherwise the courts will only consider the claim if it constitutes "plain error" (Ferdico, 1996, p. 73). It is possible for a lower court ruling to be upheld even if an appellate court finds an error in the lower court trial proceedings. The "harmless error doctrine" holds that small, insignificant errors that are believed to have little or no impact on the outcome of a case are not grounds for overturning a court decision. Scheb and Scheb (2003) note that technical errors cited by defendants are typically recognized by appellate courts as harmless and unworthy of reversing a trial court decision.

The appeal procedure varies by state, although it typically involves the filing of a notice to appeal (which must be conducted within a short period of time, usually 30–60 days); preparing and transmitting the trial court record (providing the appellate court with an account of the proceedings in the trial); the identification of the portion of the trial that is to be considered, and the filing of briefs (which are written arguments that set "forth the party's view of the facts of the case, the issues raised on appeal, and the precedents supporting their position" [Neubauer, 2005, p. 401]); oral arguments regarding the issue of consideration; a written opinion following the judicial deliberation; and a disposition, or outcome.

Options available to appellate courts include affirming, or upholding, the lower court decision; reversing the lower court decision; and reversing and remanding the lower court decision, in which the lower court decision is changed, although the case is returned to trial court for further arguments and another verdict. A "reverse and remand" decision by an appellate court would appear to violate constitutional protections from double jeopardy, however, defendants waive their right against double jeopardy upon filing an appeal. Neubauer (2005, p. 397) notes that "Appellate courts were created partly because of the belief that several heads are better than one," adding that "They operate as multi-member or collegial bodies, with decisions made by a group of judges" (p. 397). The number of judges varies among appellate courts.

Appellate courts uphold lower court decisions if they find no or harmless errors committed at trial. If the appeal was heard in an intermediate court of appeal, the case may then be appealed to the state's highest court of appeal. The appeal may be submitted to the U.S. Supreme Court for consideration if it was initially heard in the state's highest court of appeal. A second appeal, for instance those made to the U.S. Supreme Court and those made to the state's highest court of appeals, is subject to discretionary review, whereas defendants have a right to a first appeal. In other words, defendants are entitled to have one appeal heard, however, subsequent appeals are at the discretion of the appellate courts. Defendants are also provided the right to an attorney at the first appeal (*Douglas v. California*, 1963), although that right does not extend to second, or discretionary, appeals (*Ross v. Moffitt*, 1974). Defendants are no longer presumed innocent while their cases are under appeal based on their conviction. Accordingly, the burden of proof shifts and it is the responsibility of the defendant to demonstrate why his or her appeal should be upheld.

Prosecutors in some jurisdictions are provided the right to appeal; however, the rights of the prosecutor are more limited than those of the defense, largely due to concerns regarding double jeopardy. Generally, prosecutors are permitted to appeal only adverse decisions prior to a jury hearing the case. Most states do not permit the prosecution to appeal a case once an acquittal is rendered. Prosecutorial appeals are offered to help establish guidelines in future cases, not to overturn an acquittal (Stuckey, et al., 2004). Among other issues, prosecutors may appeal a judge's ruling in suppression hearings or the punishment imposed.

Most criminal cases do not undergo appellate review, simply because most cases are settled via plea bargaining. Furthermore, not all cases eligible for appeal are appealed. Most appeals are heard in state appellate courts, and most appeals are upheld. In his study of appellate court decision making, Neubauer (1991, p. 85) found that "Appellants convicted of nonviolent offenses, in which a relatively light sentence was imposed, are the most likely to win on appeal. Conversely, appellants convicted of violent crimes and sentenced to a long prison term are the least likely to gain a reversal." Williams (1991) found that a defendant's race played a significant role in determining whether a trial court decision was affirmed in cases where a judge departed from the sentence recommended by guidelines.

Many misdemeanor cases are tried before a judge in local courts that are not considered courts of record (i.e., a transcript is not made for each case and no record is available for appellate review). Those convicted of misdemeanors, however, are generally entitled to appellate review of their case. A trial *de novo,* or "new trial," is conducted when no record has been made of the initial proceedings. The trial *de novo* is conducted in a trial court of superior jurisdiction (Scheb & Scheb, 2003).

Most people recognize our courts of appeal as restricted to reviewing only trial court decisions, however, 15 states have a process by which defendants may request review of their sentence. Some states permit prosecutors to appeal sentences they believe are too lenient (Territo et al., 2004).

State and federal statutes generally discuss criteria for the release of convicted defendants pending appellate review of their case. The granting of bail following a conviction and pending appellate review is not a constitutional right; instead, post-conviction bail is at the discretion of the trial court judge. Judges consider several factors in granting or denying bail for the convicted, including whether the appeal involves a debatable point of law; whether the appeal was made in good faith; the defendant's prior record; the defendant's ties to family and their community; and the severity of the sentence imposed (Scheb & Scheb, 2003).

POST-CONVICTION REVIEW

State and federal inmates have several avenues through which they may challenge their convictions once all opportunities for appeal are exhausted. Neubauer (2005) notes that such post-conviction remedies differ from appeals in several ways. First, only those in prison may file for post-conviction review. Second, the issue raised in a petition must address constitutional issues as opposed to technical issues. Third, the issues raised in filing for post-conviction review may be broader than those addressed during appeal (e.g., claiming constitutional protections that emerged since the trial verdict). Furthermore, inmates can file an unlimited number of post-conviction petitions, yet there's only a limited number of courts to which they can appeal.

Similar to an appeal is a writ of *habeas corpus* in federal court, through which inmates claim violations of their constitutional rights and challenge the fact or duration of their confinement (Ferdico, 1996). Territo and colleagues (2004, p. 419) describe *habeas corpus* as "an ancient common-law device that permits judges to review the legality of someone's confinement. The writ is purely procedural; it gives only the right to a hearing. It has no bearing on the substance of the issue or the charge."

State inmates can file *habeas corpus* petitions, or similar petitions, for post-conviction relief in state courts according to most state statutes. State inmates may also file with federal courts should they wish to address federal constitutional issues. Federal courts can require states to retry or resentence an inmate following the court's decision that the inmate's constitutional rights were violated, or the judge may simply release the inmate from confinement.

Inmates historically experienced difficulty gaining writs of *habeas corpus* simply because they were required to exhaust all levels of appeals at the state level prior to applying for review with the U.S. Supreme Court. Things changed following the decision in *Fay v. Noia* (1963), which required federal courts to hear *habeas corpus* petitions from all state inmates, regardless of whether or not they properly filed appeals at the state level. The decision resulted in an increase of around 2,000 petitions around the time of *Fay* to just under 25,000 in the 1980s (Gaines & Miller, 2003). Critics argued that the increased number of petitions, of which less than 2% were successful, were clogging the federal courts and prolonging the execution of capital punishment cases. Congress, the U.S. Supreme Court, and U.S. presidents would eventually limit *habeas corpus* avenues (Gaines & Miller, 2000), for instance, through the "Antiterrorism and Effective Death Penalty Act of 1996," which, among other things, curtails the number of *habeas corpus* petitions state inmates may file in federal court and places a one-year deadline for state inmates filing a federal *habeas corpus* petition.

Research on the processing of *habeas corpus* petitions in 18 Federal District Courts found that ineffective assistance of counsel (e.g., defense counsel failure to cross-examine a witness) was the impetus behind most *habeas corpus* petitions. Furthermore, it was found that most *habeas corpus* petitions were filed by prisoners convicted of violent crimes and given severe sentences. Very few (about 2%) *habeas corpus* petitions resulted in outcomes favorable to the prisoners who filed them (Hanson & Daley, 1995). Such a low percentage is expected given the late stage in criminal case processing at which post-conviction review occurs. In other words, many individuals have considered the merits of the case at this point in case processing, beginning with the arresting police officer through the appellate court judges who upheld the lower court conviction.

WRAP-UP

Post-conviction review of James's case failed to benefit James in any manner. As a result, he is set to serve his sentence for the armed robbery of Jane. Interestingly, the appellate court ruled that the lower court judge should have permitted the testimony from James's friend who could verify James's location at someplace other than the crime scene. However, the appellate court ruled that the testimony of James's friend would have little effect on the outcome of the case, in other words, the court ruled it a harmless error by the judge. James's *habeas corpus* petition was denied on merits, similar to the manner in which 35% of all *habeas corpus* petitions are disposed.

Point–Counterpoint

It is argued that defendants are provided too many avenues to appeal. Others note the significance of appeals. *Should we provide fewer avenues of appeal for those who have been convicted of a crime?*

Yes: Our crowded courts provide evidence of our need to limit the number of appeals available to those convicted of a crime. To begin, the criminal justice system makes numerous efforts throughout case processing to protect the rights of the accused. Providing extensive avenues of appeal for those convicted of a crime extends these protections too far.

Extended avenues of appeals enable convicts to delay justice, particularly in the case of capital murder cases where appeals are extensive. Offering convicts the right to appeal their conviction in several courts, among other things, wastes precious court resources, particularly since most trial court decisions are upheld.

No: Restricting the number of appeals available to those convicted of a crime is contrary to the fundamental ideals upon which our system of justice was built. The criminal justice system provides individuals protections throughout case processing, so why stop protecting individual rights at what could be considered the most crucial point in case processing? Appeals provide the important functions of correcting courtroom mistakes, establishing criminal justice policy, promoting consistency in the courts, and deterring judicial misconduct. Limiting the number of appeals will negatively affect each of these functions. Our criminal justice system was created with concern for the due process rights of the accused and we should continue recognizing, not abandoning, that concern.

SUGGESTED READING

Chapper, J., & Hanson, R. (1990). *Intermediate appellate courts: Improving case processing.* Williamsburg, VA: National Center for State Courts.

Hanson, R. A., & Daley, H. W. K. (1995, September). *Federal habeas corpus review: Challenging state court criminal convictions* (NCJ 155504). Washington, DC: U.S. Department of Justice, Bureau of Justice Statistics.

Neubauer, D. W. (1991). Winners and losers: Dispositions of criminal appeals before the Louisiana supreme court. *Justice Quarterly, 8*(1), pp. 85–105.

Smith, M. B. E. (1997). Do appellate courts regularly cheat? *Criminal Justice Ethics, 16*(2), pp. 11–19.

Williams, J. J. (1991). Predicting decisions rendered in criminal appeals. *Journal of Criminal Justice, 19,* pp. 463–469.

CRITICAL THINKING EXERCISES

1. Assume you are hired by the state to reorganize the state appellate court system with the goals of greater effectiveness and efficiency. How would you restructure the appellate process?

2. Create a one-page information sheet containing a bulleted list of items you believe those convicted of a crime should know prior to appealing their case. Prioritize the information with the most important items listed at the top of the list.

3. What criteria do trial court judges consider in determining whether or not to release a convicted defendant pending appeal of their case? Does this seem fair? What possible injustices do you see with regard to current practices of post-conviction bail?

SHORT ESSAY QUESTIONS

1. What are the primary difficulties faced by appellants who wish to have their convictions overturned?

2. How do appellate courts differ from trial courts?

3. What is *habeas corpus* and how does it relate to post-conviction release?

4. Discuss the sequence of events involved in processing a trial court appeal.

5. What dispositional options are available to appellate courts?

CORRECTIONS

11

PROBATION

James received a prison sentence for his latest conviction. He earlier served 18 months on probation for a felony conviction. While on probation, James was required to maintain steady employment, submit to random drug testing, and check in with his probation officer on a regular basis, in addition to several other requirements. James successfully met the terms of his probation and completed his sentence without any blemishes. Unfortunately, the rehabilitative aspect of probation had little effect on James, as he fell back into his criminal ways soon after the probation supervision ended. James admitted that the lack of pressure to "stay clean" following his probation encouraged his return to criminal behavior.

Probation is "the conditional freedom granted by a judicial officer to an alleged or adjudged adult or juvenile offender, as long as the person meets certain conditions of behavior" (Rush, 2003, p. 285). It can be traced back in the United States to 1841 when John Augustus assisted minor offenders. Augustus, a shoemaker by trade, offered bail for the release of petty criminals and would monitor their actions in the community. At the court appearance, Augustus would describe the probationer's behavior while released in the community. His practice of vouching for petty criminals and monitoring them in the community is the basis for modern probation practices. As an alternative to incarceration, probation is an attractive sentence for many offenders. A primary purpose of probation is to provide supervision for offenders living in the community.

Probation is a front-end strategy in which judges impose conditions on offenders in lieu of incarceration. Conditions could include, for example, submitting to random drug tests, obeying curfews, reporting to a probation officer on a regular basis, and avoiding particular individuals or locations. Probation may be combined with other sanctions such as fines and restitution. Judges often impose a prison sentence following a guilty verdict and suspend the sentence in lieu of having the offender reside in the community on probation. Should the offender violate the terms of probation, he or she would be accountable for their actions and subject to additional penalties. Probation is one of the few sentences that provide sentencing authorities great flexibility in addressing the concerns of offenders, particularly in the sense that the punishment can be closely tailored to the needs of the offender.

The terms *probation* and *parole* are often incorrectly used synonymously. They are similar in that both involve offender supervision in the community. They differ primarily in that parole is a back-end strategy; it is imposed following a period of incarceration (see Champion, 1999, for additional ways in which probation and parole differ). Most probationers do not serve time in jail or prison; rather, they live in the community under guidelines set forth for them by a probation agency. There are several variations of probation (e.g., shock probation and split sentencing) in which the offender first serves a short period of incarceration followed by time on probation. These and related sanctions are discussed in Chapter 12 as intermediate sanctions, or sanctions viewed as more serious than probation yet less serious than incarceration.

75

FUNCTIONS OF PROBATION

The two primary functions of probation are supervision and investigation. Investigation concerns the preparation and presentation of a presentence investigation report (PSI) for judges in sentencing hearings. Supervision refers to what most people associate with probation: monitoring offenders in the community. Clear and Dammer (2000) suggest the two primary functions (supervision and investigation) come into conflict when supervision is neglected at the expense of PSI reports. This sometimes occurs because the reports are more easily evaluated and visible to superiors than are supervision efforts. To address this issue, some large probation agencies designate probation officers to assume either investigation or supervision duties.

Clear and Cole (2003, p. 200) identify the informal nature of the supervisory aspect of probation "as a complex interaction between officers (who vary in style, knowledge, and philosophy) and offenders (who vary in responsiveness and need for supervision) in a bureaucratic organization that imposes significant formal and informal constraints on the work." The supervision aspect of probation can be categorized in three areas: the written conditions of probation, probationer reporting, and enforcing the orders of the court (Clear & Dammer, 2000). The conditions of probation include the restrictions placed on the offender while on probation. Standard conditions apply to all probation cases, while special conditions may be imposed on an as-needed, case-by-case basis.

Reporting is a vital aspect of probation, as it involves probationers and probation officers coming into contact either in an office or in the field. Historically, the frequency of contacts was, in large, at the discretion of the probation officer. Recently, however, standardized practices for probation reporting sometimes limit probation officer discretion and require specific reporting requirements (Clear & Dammer, 2000). The final component of probation supervision involves enforcing the terms of probation. This requires probation officers to properly handle cases in which probationers commit new offenses or technical violations, or behaviors that are not criminal; however, they violate the terms of the probation. Probation officers have the power to avoid involving a judge in minor infractions, although their level of discretion decreases as the severity of the violation increases.

Champion (1999) discusses the functions of probation as they pertain to its underlying philosophy of rehabilitation. Particularly, he notes that probation maintains the primary functions of (1) crime control, (2) community reintegration, (3) rehabilitation, (4) punishment, and (5) deterrence. With such a vast array of functions, it is little wonder there currently exists confusion and uncertainty regarding the particular role of probation.

Champion (1999) notes that probation serves the function of crime control through supervision provided by probation officers. The extent of crime control provided by probation officers is questionable, however, as supervising the increasing number of probationers has proven difficult. Probation officers are increasingly faced with large caseloads resulting in less supervision. Community reintegration is facilitated by offenders living in the community. Through their ability to maintain employment and family ties, among other things, probationers do not face many of the same reentry problems as inmates. Probationers are able to maintain employment and contact with their families, make restitution, and take advantage of treatment, counseling, and other services that may otherwise be unavailable to them in prison. Rehabilitation is also more likely for several reasons, not the least of which is the protection of probationers from the influence of jail or prison environments (Glaser, 1995). Probation can also be recognized as punishment, as probationers face many restrictions on their day-to-day activities. Finally, probation functions as a deterrent simply because being supervised in the community restricts one's freedoms.

PROBATIONERS

The effectiveness of probation is strongly determined by the offender's response to supervision (Clear & Cole, 2003). Probation is more effective when offenders adopt and respond favorably to their status as a probationer. How they respond to the probation officer's supervisory powers strongly influences the probationer's behavior, as it is important for those on probation to remember that they remain under government supervision while in the community. Not being confined 24 hours a day sometimes leads offenders to forget they're under correctional supervision. Clear and Cole (2003, p. 198) note that "probationers . . . commonly resent their status, even when most people think they should be grateful for 'another chance.'"

A report on probation and parole in the United States identified over 4 million men and women on probation at the end of 2003, representing a 1.2% increase during the year. This growth was less than half the 2.9% average annual growth since 1995 (Glaze & Palla, 2004). Four states had increases of over 10%. The probation supervision rate at the beginning of 2004 was 1,876 probationers per 100,000 adult residents, or about 1 out of every 53 adults. The report added that an equal percentage (49%) of probationers were convicted of felonies and misdemeanors, with 2% convicted of other infractions. The greatest percentage of probationers were white (56%) males (77%) (Glaze & Palla, 2004).

Probationers generally share characteristics distinct from those sentenced to incarceration, and their crimes are often less harmful. For instance, probationers are more likely to be first-time or low-risk offenders. Females are more likely than males to be considered for probation, and those without a history of substance abuse problems are more likely than those with abuse problems to be granted probation. Finally, probation is more likely if the offender is convicted of a crime that does not involve harm to a victim, and/or doesn't involve weapons (Champion, 1999).

CONDITIONS OF PROBATION

Probation is often recognized by the public as being soft on crime, unresponsive to victim concerns, and misguided in attempts to rehabilitate violent offenders (e.g., Petersilia, 1997). In response, some judges are imposing tougher probation sentences, and are requiring greater monitoring of those on probation (Petersilia, 1997).

Clear and Cole (2003) note that probation supervision ultimately can be recognized within the context of a bureaucratic organization, which imposes informal and formal conditions upon probationers. Formal constraints are guided by courts and/or the law, and placed within three categories: standard conditions, punitive conditions, and treatment conditions. Standard conditions are general constraints imposed on all probationers (e.g., accountability to probation officers, remaining employed, notifying their probation officer regarding any change of address). Punitive conditions are imposed on probationers to increase the severity or restrictiveness of their sentence (e.g., fines, restitution, community service), and can be recognized within the context of the "get tough" approach to crime. Treatment conditions target particular needs of the probationer, and maintain a rehabilitative approach to probation. These conditions could include substance abuse treatment, anger management courses, and general counseling requirements (Clear & Cole, 2003). Current probation practices have become increasingly punitive in nature. It would seem that imposing numerous and/or stringent conditions on a probationer would increase control over the offender. However, an increased number of conditions often results in the trivialization of all conditions, while more stringent conditions increases the likelihood of probationers violating the terms of their probation agreement.

The decentralized administration of probation is demonstrative of correctional practices and, more generally, criminal justice in the United States. Three models of administration govern probation services in the United States. A state-level agency is responsible for probation services in the *state-administered model,* while local officials at the county or city levels administer probation services in the *locally administered model.* The *mixed model* includes representatives from the state and local levels working together to provide probation services, with state-level officials charged with setting standards and regulating the provisions of probationers and localities generally tasked with the day-to-day operations of probation services (McCarthy, McCarthy, & Leone, 2001).

TERMINATING PROBATION

Probation ends in one of two ways: the probationer successfully completes the terms of the probation, or the probationer misbehaves and probation is revoked. Most (59%) adults leaving probation in 2003 successfully met the terms of their probation (Glaze & Palla, 2004). Misbehavior includes probationers committing a crime or technical violation while on release. Probation revocation can be controversial in that some individuals may serve time in prison for behavior that is not necessarily illegal (i.e., a technical violation). For instance, one could have their probation revoked for failing to notify their probation officer regarding a change of address. Glaze and Palla (2004) note that 16% of probationers in 2003 were discharged from probation because of a rule violation or a new offense. Four percent were discharged because they absconded. Earlier research noted that most (74%) incarcerated probation violators were convicted on a new offense, while only about a quarter (26%) were incarcerated following a technical violation (Cohen, 1995).

Because probation revocation contains such a significant change in status for the probationer (from probationer to prisoner), courts provide several due process protections for probationers during revocation hearings. For instance, in *Mempa v. Rhey* (1967), the U.S. Supreme Court ruled that defendants could not receive a sentence after probation revocation without the assistance of an attorney to represent them. In *Gagnon v. Scarpelli* (1973), the Supreme Court clarified the probation revocation hearing process. Particularly, the process involves three steps. First, the facts of the case are reviewed at the preliminary hearing to determine if there is probable cause to believe a violation occurred. Next, the hearing is conducted and the facts of the case are heard and a decision is rendered. The probation department presents evidence to support the allegation, and the probationer is provided an opportunity to refute the evidence. Among other rights, the defendant maintains "the right to see written notice of the charges and the disclosure of evidence of the violation, to testify and to present witnesses and evidence to contradict the allegations, to cross-examine adversarial witnesses, and to be heard by a neutral and detached officer" (Clear & Cole, 2003, p. 208). Sentencing is the third stage of the revocation hearing. In this stage a judge decides whether to impose a term of incarceration and, if so, for how long.

EFFECTIVENESS OF PROBATION

Probation seems least effective for adults convicted of felonies, with one study reporting 65% of probationers rearrested (three-quarters of the arrests for "the crimes most threatening to public safety"), with 51% reconvicted within 40 months (Petersilia, Turner, Kahan, & Peterson, 1985, p. vii). Morgan (1993) identified several factors most frequently identified in the research literature as significantly associated with failure on probation: employment status, prior criminal record, low income, age, sex, and marital status. Morgan notes that unemployed or underemployed young males with a criminal record and low income face the greatest chances of failure. Some suggest probation could be more effective with "increased attention to, and evaluation of, those screening tools designed to assess risk to the public and the needs of the offender" (McCarthy et al., 2001, p. 100).

Probation officer caseloads are the target of criticism as they've expanded with the increased use of probation. Many individuals and groups (e.g., the President's Crime Commission on Law Enforcement and Administration of Justice) have called for small probation caseloads; however, we've recently seen average caseloads of over 100 probationers per probation officer. Caseloads of 250 or more clients are the norm in some jurisdictions (e.g., Schmalleger, 2005). Such high ratios of clients per probation officer seemingly results in watered-down supervision.

Probation provides many benefits and remains a popular criminal sanction. Its popularity will increase as prisons become increasingly overcrowded and more jurisdictions require probationers to pay fees for their supervision. Governments faced with budget crunches are most likely to view probation as an attractive alternative to incarceration. Some suggest probation could be enhanced to further meet the needs of society. For instance, Petersilia (1997, p. 7) offers the following suggestions to achieve greater crime control over probationers:

- Provide adequate financial resources to deliver treatment programs that have been shown to work.

- Combining *both* treatment and surveillance in probation programs and focusing them on appropriate offender subgroups.

- Work to garner more public support by convincing citizens that probation sanctions are punitive and in the long run cost-effective.

- Convince the judiciary that offenders will be held accountable for their behavior.

- Give priority to research addressing probation's most pressing problems.

These suggestions certainly offer much toward increasing the effectiveness of current probation services.

WRAP-UP

Probation currently faces many challenges as we begin the 21st century. For instance, many people feel probation is a slap on the wrist of offenders who deserve greater punishment. The criminal justice system continuously faces public criticism whenever a probationer reoffends. Some critics use particular cases involving unsuccessful probationers to cite the limitations of probation and the criminal justice system in general. Considering that probation is the most commonly imposed correctional sanction and its use continues to increase, professionals within the criminal justice system need to explain to the public why so many offenders receive probation instead of incarceration. If indeed probation is more than a slap on the wrist, criminal justice professionals should explain how and why.

Point–Counterpoint

Probation is controversial in the sense that some see it as too soft on criminals, although others appreciate the contributions of probation, including the rehabilitative effects and easing the burden of overcrowded prisons. *Should we eliminate probation as it is currently practiced?*

Yes: Probation as it is currently used does little to meet the goals of criminal sentencing. Probationers are not punished, incapacitated, nor deterred, and there's little rehabilitation occurring. Probation has become so watered down that the protection of society has been compromised with too many dangerous, poorly supervised criminals not being properly monitored.

Probation sentences for serious felonies make a mockery of justice. What message is being sent to potential criminals? There's too much discretion in probation. For instance, judges maintain the power to impose probation, determine the conditions of probation, revoke probation, and so on. Probation officers maintain the power to closely supervise some offenders, yet "look the other way" for other offenders.

No: Abolish probation? What will we do with the *millions* who are currently being supervised in the community? Besides, there are many benefits to probation, including the lower cost of probation (about $3,000 annually per probationer) compared to incarceration (over $20,000 annually per offender in most states; Clear & Dammer, 2000). Furthermore, probation facilitates rehabilitation and restoration by helping offenders maintain ties with the community, and enables them to work and ultimately pay restitution as necessary. It also eliminates the label of "inmate" associated with incarceration and limits the offender's exposure to prison life. In sum, probation is cheaper and increases the likelihood of offender rehabilitation. One could view discretion within probation as a contribution, as it permits those involved to tailor practices and sentences as necessary.

SUGGESTED READING

Geerken, M. R., & Hayes, H. D. (1993). Probation and parole: Public risk and the future of incarceration alternatives. *Criminology, 31*(4), pp. 549–564.

Johnson, S. J. (1998). Probation: My profession, my lifetime employment, my passion. *Crime & Delinquency, 44*(1), pp. 117–120.

Kingsnorth, R. F., MacIntosh, R. C., & Sutherland, S. (2002). Criminal charge or probation violation? Prosecutorial discretion and implications for research in criminal court processing. *Criminology, 40*(3), pp. 553–577.

Morgan, K. D. (1993, June). Factors influencing probation outcome: A review of the literature. *Federal Probation*, pp. 23–29.

Panzarella, R. (2002). Theory and practice of probation on bail in the report of John Augustus. *Federal Probation, 66*(3) pp. 38–42.

CRITICAL THINKING EXERCISES

1. What could be done to improve current probation practices? Are these changes realistic given society's current concern for a more punitive approach toward crime?
2. Use the Internet to visit the probation agency of your state or county. What administrative model does it follow? Compare your jurisdiction's organization of probation with a neighboring jurisdiction.
3. Use the Internet to identify the qualifications to become a probation officer. Compare these qualifications to those required to become a police officer. What are the differences? Should there be differences? Explain why or why not.

SHORT ESSAY QUESTIONS

1. What are the two primary functions of probation? How do these functions relate to probation's underlying philosophy of rehabilitation?
2. Identify and discuss the three models of probation administration. Which do you feel is most effective? Why?
3. Identify and discuss the steps involved in probation revocation. Design what you believe would be a more effective model.
4. Who is on probation? Describe the probation population.
5. Who is most likely to succeed on probation? What reasons might explain why these groups do better than others while on probation?

12 INTERMEDIATE SANCTIONS

At the sentencing hearing, James's attorney made a strong argument for James to be considered for several intermediate sanctions. The attorney reasoned that although probation is not a feasible option in James's case primarily because of the prior convictions and the violent nature of the current offense, incarceration would do little to address the problems underlying James's criminal behavior. He suggested James be placed on intensive probation supervision or be sentenced to house arrest in conjunction with electronic monitoring. The attorney argued that James would have a much greater chance of making restitution and avoiding future criminal behavior if he was permitted to serve his time in the community. The sentencing judge agreed that community supervision could certainly help James control his behavior, however; the judge stated that James's recent violent behavior and his poor criminal record leave him unsuitable for either sanction.

Intermediate sentences are more severe than traditional probation, yet less severe than incarceration. They provide sentencing bodies flexibility in sentencing and help address concerns that probation for some is too lenient while incarceration is unnecessary. Intermediate sanctions are considered more attractive than incarceration simply because they are less expensive than incarceration, help keep offenders in the community where they can maintain employment and family ties, and offer flexibility for sentencing bodies to tailor sentences to meet particular offender needs.

McCarthy and colleagues (2001) identify three objectives of intermediate sanctions. The first and foremost objective of intermediate sanctions is to protect the community. Corrections officials use risk assessments to determine suitability for various intermediate sanctions. Second, intermediate sanctions expand the range of punishments for convicted offenders, helping sentencing bodies meet offender needs while maintaining the ideals of justice. Intermediate sanctions provide alternatives to probation and incarceration that can be tailored to most effectively achieve justice. With intermediate sanctions sentencing bodies have options through being able to use multiple sanctions (e.g., intensive supervision probation *and* restitution). Third, intermediate sanctions are designed to help reduce prison costs. Intermediate sanctions are increasingly appealing as many states see substantial portions of their budgets consumed by prison costs.

The range of intermediate sanctions is not consistent among jurisdictions. In other words, what is available in one state may not be in another. Among the more commonly used intermediate sanctions are day reporting centers; shock probation and shock parole; shock incarceration; intensive probation supervision; and home confinement and electronic monitoring.

DAY REPORTING CENTERS

Day reporting centers (DRCs) are among the newest intermediate sanctions. They provide services, including treatment and surveillance, to offenders living in the community. Day reporting centers enable offenders to live at home or in community-supervised residences while they regularly attend self-help programs.

Offenders sentenced to day reporting are required to report each day to carry out the provisions of their sentence. These provisions may range from requiring offenders to remain at the center for a designated number of hours per day to simply requiring offenders to report to the center daily for drug testing. Day reporting centers incorporate a variety of correctional methods and programs such as parenting and life skills, counseling and education programs, drug testing, and meetings with probation officers. DRCs provide more of a rehabilitative component than do many other correctional alternatives, particularly in the sense that various programs can be offered within the centers. One study in Cook County, Illinois, found that a DRC for drug-using offenders notably helped offenders reduce their drug use, increased the likelihood of offenders appearing for court dates, and decreased their likelihood of being arrested on new charges (McBride & VanderWaal, 1997).

SHOCK PROBATION AND SHOCK PAROLE

Some states permit shock probation or shock parole in which offenders serve a brief period of incarceration followed by a period of probation. The change in status from prisoner to probationer comes unexpectedly to the offender who anticipated serving a longer period of incarceration. Specifically, those who are initially sentenced to incarceration serve a brief period in jail or prison and are then brought before a judge who reconsiders the original sentence imposed on the offender. Judges consider the offender's behavior while incarcerated and then, unexpectedly, sentence the offender to probation. Shock probation is similar to split sentencing, however, those receiving shock probation anticipated a longer stint in prison; they unexpectedly received probation. Those receiving a split sentence are more aware of their circumstances than those receiving shock probation. The purpose of shock probation/parole is to "shock" the offender into a life without crime. The "scare" they may have experienced during the brief period of incarceration hopefully acts as a deterrent to future criminal behavior.

Shock probation and shock parole reduce the costs of incarceration, enable offenders to maintain community ties, and can be an effective rehabilitative approach. The only difference between shock probation and shock parole is that the judiciary makes the early release decision in the former, while a parole board or a representative from a parole agency makes the early release decision in the latter.

SHOCK INCARCERATION

Shock incarceration is a popular sanction that typically involves young, first-time offenders undergoing strict military discipline, including physical training conducted at a boot camp. Shock incarceration is often associated with juvenile corrections, although adults are also sentenced to boot camps. Although shock incarceration programs vary in nature, they are all based on the belief that offenders can be "shocked" out of a life of crime. An overriding goal of boot camp administrators is to "break" the offender and then rebuild him or her with positive attributes such as respect for authority, respect for themselves, and self-discipline. It is hoped that this will reduce the likelihood of future involvement in crime and delinquency. Boot camps typically last 90–180 days during which drill instructors attempt to shock campers into a life absent of crime and delinquency. The tough, militaristic approach is often supplemented by education, job training, and general life skills. "Some programs . . . include educational and training components, counseling sessions, and treatment for special-needs populations, while others devote little or no time to therapeutic activities" (Senna & Siegel, 2002, p. 500). Boot camps maintain three primary goals: reducing prison costs, reducing prison crowding, and reducing recidivism (Burns, 1996).

Boot camps are attractive to policymakers who wish to appear tough on crime. The idea of having drill instructors "break" young individuals through intimidation and physical requirements coupled with treatment services is attractive to much of the public. However, research on boot camps provides mixed evaluative results and their popularity may be fading. For instance, Gaines and Miller (2003, p. 425) noted that "After a two-decade-long honeymoon period, however, many criminal justice participants are questioning whether boot camps deliver on all of their promises."

State-run boot camps are often located on the grounds of larger correctional facilities, which facilitates the sharing of particular services and programs. Those in boot camp, however, are segregated from the prison population. Local sheriff's agencies and county correctional offices run many boot camps. Local and county-run programs tend to be shorter in duration and smaller than the state-run camps (McCarthy et al., 2001).

INTENSIVE SUPERVISION PROBATION

Intensive supervision probation (ISP) truly reflects what much of the public expects from probation: close supervision of the offender in the community with stringent restrictions placed on the offender. ISP, which relies on surveillance and restrictions, is primarily designed to "protect the community and deter the offender from law-breaking or violation of the conditions of release" (McCarthy et al., 2001, p. 166). To do so, "most ISPs provide small caseloads with multiple face-to-face contacts with offenders, random and unannounced drug tests, and stringent enforcement of probation (or parole) conditions" (p. 166). ISP has become increasingly popular in the past decade, with all states having ISP as an option by 1990. About 2–4% of offenders receive ISP; however, its use at the federal level has been hampered by sentencing guidelines that offer no unclear role of ISPs (McCarthy et al., 2001).

It is unclear whether ISPs offer a solid alternative to incarceration and probation. Petersen and Palumbo (1997) note that most research suggests that ISP is not cost-effective and doesn't affect recidivism without a treatment component. They add that many programs offer little to no treatment services. Most evaluations of ISP programs find that the strict supervision and greater overall restrictions largely contribute to offenders violating the terms of their ISP at a higher rate than do those on traditional probation. Nevertheless, "ISP has become popular among probation administrators, judges, and prosecutors because it presents a 'tough' image of community supervision and addresses the problem of prison crowding" (Cole & Smith, 2004, p. 451).

HOME CONFINEMENT AND ELECTRONIC MONITORING

The use of home confinement and electronic monitoring as a sanction drew widespread attention recently when celebrity Martha Stewart returned home from spending 5 months in federal prison and was required to serve another 5 months under house arrest. Home confinement (or house arrest) requires offenders to remain within the confines of their home during specific hours of each day. Monitoring home confinement ranges "from evening curfew to detention during all nonworking hours to continuous incarceration at home. Monitoring techniques may range from periodic visits or telephone calls to continuous monitoring with electronic equipment" (Rackmill, 1994, p. 46). Restrictions for those confined to their homes include *curfews,* which require offenders to be in their homes during certain parts of each day; *home detention,* which requires offenders to remain at home at all times, with the exception of outings related to education, counseling, and employment; and *home incarceration,* which requires offenders to remain in their homes at all times except in cases involving medical emergencies (Gaines & Miller, 2003).

Those sentenced to home confinement face the same restrictions as probationers, and are sometimes permitted to leave their home to attend school, work, counseling, and other approved locations. Conditions are often electronically enforced through telephone calls, field visits, and/or a monitoring device (the most common form being an ankle bracelet), which sends an electronic message identifying the offender's entrance or exit from their home. The active version of electronic monitoring uses a monitoring device that continuously sends a signal to a probation office. The probation officer will know the offender left the designated premises once the signal is lost. A variation of the monitoring device, or what is recognized as the passive version, requires the offender to place the ankle or wrist device into a verifier box, which, often along with voice identification, confirms the offender's identity.

The use of electronic monitoring and home confinement steadily grew throughout the 1980s and 1990s. Currently, home confinement is used in all 50 U.S. states for both juveniles and adults, and most of the approximately 18,000 federal offenders sentenced to home confinement in 2002 were under electronic monitoring programs (U.S. Probation and Pretrial Services, 2003).

The use of electronic monitoring demonstrates how technology can assist the criminal justice system. Technological advances in this area seem promising. For instance, voice recognition systems, satellite tracking devices, and biometrics lead some to believe home confinement with electronic monitoring could prove to be a quite effective intermediate sanction.

In addition to the intermediate sanctions discussed above, one could add fines, restitution, community service, halfway houses, substance abuse treatment, and drug court intervention. Split sentencing is also considered an intermediate sanction as it can meet the criteria of being more punitive than probation yet less severe than incarceration. Particularly, split sentences may be an option to sentencing bodies who feel a combination of probation and incarceration best suits a particular offender. For instance, a judge may sentence an offender to 3 months in jail followed by 24 months on probation.

WRAP-UP

Tonry (1998, p. 700) found the research on intermediate sanctions "seemingly disheartening," noting that the sanctions do not seem to reduce corrections costs, recidivism, nor prison crowding. Nor do they seem to provide public safety. He sees a future for intermediate sanctions, however, should the U.S. clear three hurdles. The first concerns the "preoccupation with absolute severity of punishment and the related widespread view that only imprisonment counts" (p. 701). The second obstacle concerns a commitment to the "just desserts" approach, which stresses finding punishments that fit the crime. Finally, Tonry sees net widening, or the expansion of correctional supervision resulting from correctional options, as a clear barrier to the effective indoctrination and use of intermediate sanctions.

The term *intermediate sanctions* is used to identify a series of sanctions that can bear little resemblance to one another; it incorporates a spectrum of sanctions, each with a different approach, differing levels of effectiveness, and varied philosophical bases. One must use caution when using the term *intermediate sanctions*, as, similar to the term *crime*, it can refer to a variety of actions that can be vaguely related.

A pressing issue with regard to intermediate sanctions concerns perceived severity of sanctions. For instance, is ISP more punitive than shock probation? Spelman (1995, p. 132) notes "that it is possible, even in the short term, to develop a punishment scheme that rationally relates the severity of the crime to the severity of the punishment." Similarly, Petersilia and Deschenes (1994, p. 306) suggest that "It is no longer necessary to equate criminal punishment solely with prison. At some level of intensity and length, intensive probation is equally severe as prison."

Intermediate sanctions must continue to find their niche in corrections and sentencing. In discussing the social construction of intermediate sanctions, Petersen and Palumbo (1997, p. 83) note the attractiveness of intermediate sanctions to the public in suggesting that they are "justifiable on the premise that they are tough punishment." Being tough, however, is not always the most effective approach. Toughness may be effective for some yet not others. We must carefully scrutinize the appropriateness and effectiveness of the options provided by intermediate sanctions and determine which offenders, under what circumstances, would benefit most.

Point–Counterpoint

Some question the efficacy of intermediate sanctions to offer more effective solutions than probation and incarceration. Others highlight the contributions of intermediate sanctions, such as their potential for rehabilitation and their flexibility. *Should sentencing bodies consider intermediate sanctions?*

Yes: The benefits of intermediate sanctions are obvious. First, they are less expensive than incarceration. In a time of financial crises, intermediate sanctions free taxpayer money from the financial burdens of prison. Furthermore, intermediate sanctions are socially cost-effective. For instance, supervising offenders in the community provides numerous benefits for all. Intermediate sanctions provide flexibility; not everyone deserves either incarceration or probation. Why should we be so shortsighted to believe that we only require two primary sanctions to achieve justice? Intermediate sanctions can satisfy the public's desire to punish without relying on incarceration; intermediate sanctions enable us to successfully punish *and* rehabilitate particular offenders.

No: We ought to stop touting the greatness of intermediate sanctions until further evaluations determine what sanctions are most effective for whom. In other words, the sanctions remain unproven as demonstrated by the inconclusive evaluation research findings with regard to most, if not all, intermediate sanctions. While the goal of reducing prison costs is undoubtedly attractive and seems most feasible via intermediate sanctions, we cannot claim a cost savings if offenders commit additional crimes while in the community and eventually end up in prison. Concerns of net widening are real, as are concerns regarding stronger nets, or the intensification of formal social control. Uncertainty regarding who is supposed to administer particular intermediate sanctions remains problematic in cases, and inadequate funding for several intermediate sanctions has contributed to lax enforcement.

SUGGESTED READING

Blomberg, T. G., & Lucken, K. (1994). Stacking the deck by piling up sanctions? *Howard Journal of Criminal Justice, 33*, pp. 62–80.

Langan, P. A. (1994). Between prison and probation: Intermediate sanctions. *Science, 264*, pp. 791–793.

McCarthy, B. R. (Ed.). (1987). *Intermediate punishments: Intensive supervision, home confinement and electronic surveillance.* Monsey, NY: Willow Tree Press.

Morris, N., & Tonry, M. (1990). *Between prison and probation: Intermediate punishments in a rational sentencing system.* New York: Oxford University Press.

Smykla, J., & Selke, W. (Eds.). (1994). *Intermediate sanctions: Sentencing in the 1990's.* Cincinnati, OH: Anderson.

CRITICAL THINKING EXERCISES

1. The current "get tough" approach to crime resulted in criminal justice officials becoming more punitive with regard to intermediate sanctions. Assume that in 10 years a reversal of the "get tough" approach occurs and society becomes more concerned with rehabilitation. Describe the likely impact on intermediate sanctions.

2. Assume you are a judge tasked with sentencing an 18-year-old, first-time, male offender convicted on one charge of trafficking cocaine. By law, you are required to impose an intermediate sanction. Which sentence do you choose and why?

3. Which intermediate sanctions do you feel are best suited for property offenders? Drug offenders? Violent offenders? Substance abusers? Be sure to provide reasons why you feel particular sanctions are best suited for these groups.

SHORT ESSAY QUESTIONS

1. What is the difference between shock probation and shock parole? What is the difference between shock probation and shock incarceration?

2. Discuss the three objectives of intermediate sanctions.

3. How does intensive supervision probation differ from traditional probation?

4. What are boot camps and what are they designed to do? In other words, what are their goals? Do you feel the boot camp regimen is appropriate in modern corrections? Why or why not?

5. What is the difference between home detention and home incarceration? Which do you feel would be most effective for white-collar criminals?

13

INCARCERATION AND CAPITAL PUNISHMENT

James's 6-year state prison sentence is to be served at a maximum security prison in his home state. He will be processed and ultimately integrated into the general prison population. James is beginning to regret his violent behavior, and at times views his upcoming prison sentence as an opportunity to make amends to society and better himself. The prison offers several rehabilitative opportunities that should benefit James. In particular, James will seek a high school equivalency diploma and computer skills to enhance his chances of living a crime-free life upon release. James plans to respect the inmate code during his stay, although he doesn't wish to get caught up in the social network of the prison society. Unfortunately for James, he will not serve time at the same prison currently housing his brother and cousin. They, too, were incarcerated for violent crimes.

Simply stated, corrections is very expensive. For instance, Stephan (2004) noted that state correctional costs increased from $15.6 billion in 1986 to $38.2 billion in 2001, an increase of 145%. The increased cost of corrections has a direct impact on all citizens, as each U.S. resident contributed $104 toward state prison costs in 2001; over twice the $49 each citizen paid in 1986 (Stephan, 2004). The bulk of resources targeted toward corrections goes toward adult correctional facilities.

As a general rule, those receiving sentences of incarceration of 12 months or more are placed in prison. Those receiving less than 12 months typically serve their penalty in jail; however, jails also incarcerate individuals in several categories, including inmates being transferred among authorities, mentally ill individuals awaiting assessment, and those awaiting trial (see Harrison & Karberg, 2004, for other categories). Incarceration is one of the most stringent sentences. Even more stringent than incarceration is capital punishment, which is reserved for the most heinous crimes and dangerous offenders.

INCARCERATION

The custodial, rehabilitation, and reintegration models of incarceration were prominent in corrections since the early 1940s (Cole & Smith, 2004). The *custodial model* dominates most maximum security prisons today through its emphasis on incapacitation, deterrence, and retribution. The focus is on security, discipline, and order. This approach was also prevalent prior to World War II. The *rehabilitation model* seeks to treat or rehabilitate offenders. This model appeared in the 1950s and continued to the 1970s when some questioned the rehabilitative abilities of corrections. Offender rehabilitation currently is not a primary consideration in most facilities. The *reintegration model* is akin to community corrections through its emphasis on maintaining ties with the community. The belief is that one should remain in contact with the outside world while incarcerated for the sake of easing the transition from prisoner to citizen (Cole & Smith, 2004).

There were 2,212,475 incarcerated persons in the United States at the end of 2003. Most (62.7%) were held in state and federal prisons. Just under one-third (31.2%) were incarcerated in local jails (Harrison & Beck, 2004). Others were located in territorial prisons, facilities under the direction of the Bureau of Immigration and Customs Enforcement, military facilities, jails in Indian country, and juvenile facilities. Private prisons are becoming more ingrained in American corrections, as noted by the 5.7% of state prison inmates, and 12.6% of federal inmates housed in private facilities at yearend 2003 (Harrison & Beck, 2004). Stephan and Karberg (2003) note that over one-third of the 460 community-based correctional facilities were privately operated in 2000.

Harrison and Beck (2004) identified 1,470,045 prisoners in state and federal correctional facilities at yearend 2003, with a 2.1% prison population growth during the year that was down from the average annual growth of 3.4% since the end of 1995. The rate of 482 sentenced inmates per 100,000 U.S. residents in 2003 was up from the rate of 411 in 1995. "About 1 in every 109 men and 1 in every 1,613 women were sentenced prisoners under the jurisdiction of State or Federal authorities" (Harrison & Beck, 2004, p. 1). Most inmates are located in state prisons.

Males constitute the bulk of American prisoners. For instance, there were only 101,179 (6.9% of prisoners) female inmates in state and federal prison at yearend 2003 (Harrison & Beck, 2004). The 2003 rate of 62 female state or federal prisoners per 100,000 residents is up from 47 female prisoners per 100,000 residents in 1995 (Harrison & Beck, 2004). Interestingly, "The number of female prisoners increased 3.6%—higher than that of men, 2.0%—during 2003" (Harrison & Beck, 2004, p. 4). Harrison and Beck (2004, p. 8) also note that the U.S. prison population is getting older, with the mean age at admission to state prison of 33, up from the mean age of 31 in 1995. They note that the underlying reasons behind the increased mean age include "a gradual rise in the age of State inmates at time of admission compounded by a sharp increase in time served in prison" (p. 8). Black inmates constituted the largest percentage of state and federal prisoners (44.1%), followed by whites (35.0%) and Hispanics (19.0%); however, there is an interesting difference between genders with regard to race. Harrison and Beck (2004) note that "At yearend 2003 black males (586,300) outnumbered white males (454,300) and Hispanic males (251,900)," however, "white females (39,107) outnumbered black females (35,050) and Hispanic females (16,172)" (p. 9).

Such a large number of prisoners brings about many associated costs. For instance, $29.5 billion of the $38.2 billion (or 77.2%) spent by correctional authorities on state correctional systems went toward adult correctional facilities in 2001 (Stephan, 2004). Stephan (2004) notes that the average operating cost of each state inmate in 2001 was $22,650 annually, or $62.05 daily. The costs per federal inmate were similar ($22,632 and $62.01, respectively). He adds that state *correctional* costs per U.S. resident increased 6.2% annually between 1986 and 2001, while state *prison* costs per resident increased 6.4% annually during that period. These increases surpass the annual increased spending in areas such health care (5.8% annual increase from 1986 through 2001), education (4.2%), and natural resources (3.3%). Despite such large increases, the $38.2 billion spent on corrections in 2001 was far less than states spent on education ($374.5 billion) and public welfare ($260.3 billion). It nevertheless suggests that a great deal of financial resources are spent on corrections, particularly on prisons. The costs of incarceration are not restricted to economics, however, as one must consider the associated costs of incarceration (e.g., societal costs).

U.S. incarceration rates have increased dramatically since the 1970s, and the number of individuals incarcerated in the United States has more than doubled since 1985. For instance, Bonczar (2003) notes that in 1974 just over 1.8 million U.S. residents (1.3% of residents) had served time in prison. That number jumped to over 5.6 million (2.7% of residents) by 2001. Bonczar (2003, p. 1) notes that "If rates of first incarceration remain unchanged, 6.6% of all persons born in the United States in 2001 will go to State or Federal prison during their lifetime, up from 5.2% in 1991, and 1.9% in 1974." Among the factors influencing current levels of incarceration are a lack of focus on rehabilitation, more punitive sentencing structures and practices, increased prison construction, the war on drugs, and greater societal frustration with crime and criminals.

The 6-year (72-month) prison sentence given to James, the character in our case study, falls below the 91-month mean state prison sentence given to felons for robbery in 2002 (Durose & Langan, 2004). Should the percentage of time served stay consistent, James can expect to serve 58% of his sentence, or about 3.5 years. The mean prison sentence given for *all* offenses in 2002 was 53 months, with inmates serving an average of 51% of their designated time. Violent offenders, on average, served 62% of an 84-month sentence, while property offenders served an average of 49% of an average 41-month sentence (Durose & Langan, 2004).

JAILS

Jails serve several functions, including detaining those who cannot make, or are not granted, pretrial release. Jails also hold convicted offenders who are awaiting sentencing; house those sentenced to incarceration for less than a year; house felons when state prisons are too overcrowded; and detain probation and parole violators who violated the terms of their agreement and await a hearing. Jails are clearly one of, if not the most, underappreciated component of criminal justice.

Discussed earlier in this work under the guise of pretrial detention, jails are recognized as "poorhouses of the twentieth century" (Goldfarb, 1975, p. 29), dumping grounds for officers engaged in social sanitation (Welch, 1994), and "the ultimate ghetto" (Thompson, 1986, p. 205). Jails remain a vital cog in the American system of justice despite these unflattering titles and an overall neglect by researchers and academics (Burns, 2002; Irwin, 1985). Irwin (1985, p. xi) argues that jails are worthy of greater attention than prison because: (1) jail-based experiences greatly influence inmates' minds; (2) many critical decisions are made while detained in jail or released on bond; (3) more people go through jails than prisons; and (4) "the jail, not the prison, imposes the cruelest form of punishment in the United States."

The limited attention to jails is due, in part, to a misunderstanding of the role of jails in the American system of justice. For instance, some people don't realize that jails hold both the guilty and those awaiting trial. For instance, actor Robert Blake, who was recently acquitted of murder in the 2001 death of his wife, spent 11 months in jail prior to being released on bond. The general public may also be unaware that jails, which are often confused with prisons, are typically operated by law enforcement agents (usually by sheriff's departments). These and other misperceptions regarding jails led Clear and Cole (2003) to note that "jails are an important part of corrections and demonstrate many complexities of the system" (p. 154). The complexity is evident in jails being directly involved with all three major components of the criminal justice system: police, courts, and corrections.

So who is in jail and why are they there? Recent numbers suggest 691,301 individuals were held in local jails at midyear 2003 (Harrison & Karberg, 2004). Some estimates place new jail admissions at 9.8 million per year (Perkins, Stephan, & Beck, 1995). James (2004) recently found that the average jail inmate is getting older, as 38% of jail inmates were age 35 or older in 2002, up from 32% in 1996. There's little difference among the types of crimes for which jail inmates were being held in 2002, as roughly the same percentage of jail inmates were charged with violent (25.4%), property (24.4%), drug (24.7%), and public-order (24.9%) offenses. Just under half (46%) of jail inmates in 2002 were on probation or parole at the time of their arrest (James, 2004). Harrison and Karberg (2004) note that the local jail population increased 3.9% from 665,475 to 691,301 between midyear 2002 and 2003. The increase was consistent with the annual average increase of 4% between midyear 1995 and midyear 2003. The annual average increase in female jail inmates (6.4%)

is notably higher than the average increase for males (3.9%) in the past decade; however, males (88.1% of the local jail population) far outnumber females (11.9%) in local jails.

With regard to race and ethnicity, Harrison and Karberg (2004) note that whites constitute 43.6% of the local jail population, followed by black (39.2%) and Hispanic (15.4%) inmates. Three out of every five local adult jail inmates (60.6%) were unconvicted at midyear 2003, while 39.4% were convicted. A sizable portion (31.2%, or 215,729) of jail inmates were housed within the 50 largest U.S. jails as of midyear 2003.

Jail inmates often do not get the medical and rehabilitative services provided in prisons, primarily because of the transient nature of the jail population. Classification, funding, overcrowding, and personnel issues are also confronting jails. Inmate classification is less of a concern to jail officials than it is to prison officials simply because less attention is given to separating jail inmates since many won't be in the facility for long periods of time. Jails are not a high priority with regard to state funding, in part because of the aforementioned underappreciation of jails. With regard to jail overcrowding, Clear and Cole (2003, p. 175) state: "The number of people confined in jails reached nearly crisis proportions in the early 1990s." Cells constructed to hold two inmates sometimes house four or five inmates, resulting in several problems. Clear and Cole (2003, p. 174) also highlight the personnel concerns in local jails, noting that "Local correctional workers are among the most poorly trained, least-educated, and worst-paid employees in the criminal justice system. Many take custodial positions on a temporary basis while awaiting an opening in the ranks of the sheriff's law enforcement officers."

PRISONS

The current "Just Desserts Era" of prisons, which began in the mid-1990s, emphasizes individual responsibility and relies heavily on punishment as a response to criminal behavior. Limited concern for rehabilitation, tougher sentences, the construction of new prisons, and increased incarceration rates are representative of the modern era of prisons. Getting tougher on inmates seems, to many, the ideal solution to crime; however, some question whether the current approach is effective. Perhaps the most obvious problem resulting from current incarceration practices is overcrowding, which negatively impacts many prisons. For instance, federal prisons were operating at 39% over capacity at yearend 2003 (Harrison & Beck, 2004).

Prisons are classified according to security levels. Maximum-security prisons hold dangerous offenders who pose the greatest threat to society. They are highly regimented and typically contain high walls and armed guards protecting the perimeter. Inmates in maximum-security prisons are provided little contact with the outside world. Medium-security prisons resemble maximum-security prisons in appearance, although the security and overall atmosphere are not as vigilant (Senna & Siegel, 2002). Inmates in medium-security prisons are permitted greater contact with the outside world than inmates in maximum-security prisons. Minimum-security prisons typically house white-collar criminals and an assortment of nonviolent offenders. The security level is much lower than at medium- and maximum-security facilities, and furloughs and visitation policies are used more liberally in minimum-security prisons. Most prisons as of midyear 2000 were minimum-security (48.8%), followed by medium-(31.2%) and maximum-security level (19.9%) (Stephan & Karberg, 2003).

Supermax prisons provide a greater level of security than maximum-security prisons by isolating inmates from society, other inmates, and prison staff. They are assuming an increasingly prominent role in American corrections. While a lack of agreement exists regarding what specifically constitutes a supermax prison (e.g., Franklin, 1998), estimates suggest that in 1997 there were between 32 and 42 states operating what could be considered a supermax prison. There is agreement, however, that supermax prisons became increasingly popular in the last decade (Briggs, Sundt, & Castellano, 2003).

Prisons are presently faced with several important issues that require attention. For instance, the increasing number of elderly inmates in U.S. prisons poses several challenges including health costs, housing issues, and providing age-appropriate services for elderly inmates (Morton, 2001). HIV/AIDS is also a concern for prison inmates and officials. Although the number of HIV-positive prisoners decreased about 5% between 2000 and 2001, the overall rate of confirmed AIDS among prisoners (0.49%) is over three times the rate in the U.S. general population (0.14%; Maruschak, 2004). Mental illness is also a concern among prisons and jails, as Dutton (1999) notes that 16% of state prison inmates and 16% of local jail inmates reported either a mental condition or an overnight stay in a mental hospital. She adds that state prison inmates reporting a mental condition were more likely than other prisoners to be imprisoned for a violent offense.

Much has been written about life in prison. Recently, Ross and Richards (2002) offered guidance for those entering prison. They noted that one's prison experience is influenced by personal characteristics and traits (e.g., age, education, physical size, criminal history, etc.), the sentence received, the crime committed, and the security level of the facility. They argued that survival in prison is based on one's understanding of, and adaptation to, the inmate code and the prison rulebook. Furthermore, Ross and Richards suggest that prison-sponsored orientation in most prisons is more of a formality than anything else, as inmates learn all they need to know about prison from other inmates. The convict code to which inmates are expected to abide is a set of rules guiding inmate behavior. Tenets of the code include minding your own business, being tough, being loyal to convicts as a group, paying debts, not breaking your word or attracting attention, not exploiting other inmates, and not snitching on other inmates (Ross & Richards, 2002). In sum, one's overall adjustment to prison and ultimate success are largely based on recognition of the nuances of prison life and the ability to avoid troubling situations.

CAPITAL PUNISHMENT

Capital punishment sparks the most heated debates in crime and justice even though it is used relatively infrequently. It is seen by some as true just desserts and by others as cruel and unusual punishment. Regardless of one's view of capital punishment, it is permitted in 38 states and at the federal level. Its application, however, is disproportionately distributed in five states, which were accountable for two-thirds of the executions between January 1, 1977, and yearend 2003. Texas (313), Virginia (89), Oklahoma (68), Missouri (61), and Florida (57) were responsible for 588 of the 885 executions during this period (Bonczar & Snell, 2004).

Capital punishment was used in a relatively liberal manner in the mid-20th century, as nearly 3,800 persons were executed in the United States between 1930 and 1967. Such practices led to concern about the constitutionality of the death penalty. With public opinion polls increasingly showing opposition, the U.S. Supreme Court suspended the use of capital punishment in 1968 and issued a moratorium on its use between 1967 and 1977 when no executions took place (Schmalleger, 2005). The Court decided in *Furman v. Georgia* (1972) that the death penalty itself was not necessarily unconstitutional; however, it was being applied in an arbitrary and capricious manner. Some states quickly moved to modify their death penalty statutes and the Court, in *Gregg v. Georgia* (1976), supported a two-stage process in which sentencing in death penalty cases occurred at a different time than the delivery of the verdict, and can include information that may not have been permitted at trial, although it may be relevant to the punishment. Executions resumed in 1977 when many states began sentencing murderers to death.

Several arguments put forth by proponents of capital punishment suggest that it:

1. Deters criminals from committing violent acts. For instance, offenders will be less likely to kill someone if they believe they face execution for murder.
2. Achieves justice through retribution. Society exacts an appropriate measure of revenge: "an eye for an eye." Victim's families can be reassured, knowing their relative's murderers received a just punishment and will not be able to kill others.
3. Prevents criminals from doing further harm. Murderers who serve life sentences pose threats to those in prison.

Proponents of capital punishment remain dissatisfied with how the penalty is applied, with particular concern regarding appeals halting the pace of executions. In response, attempts were made to limit the number and length of appeals prisoners can file.

Opponents believe the death penalty lingers as a barbaric practice from an earlier, less civilized society. They note that most other developed democracies in the world don't execute criminals. In addition, opponents challenge claims that capital punishment reduces crime. They further suggest that:

1. There is no clear evidence of the death penalty as a deterrent. Many people who kill aren't thinking rationally (e.g., they're drunk, under the influence of drugs, and/or mentally ill). In turn, they do not consider the threat of capital punishment when committing their crime.
2. It is wrong for a government to intentionally kill its citizens. The message being sent is that life is cheap and violence is an appropriate response to violence.
3. The death penalty is still applied in a discriminatory fashion. Minorities and the poor are disadvantaged with regard to capital punishment.
4. Innocent people are convicted of crimes. Numerous individuals have been removed from death row after demonstrating their innocence.
5. Some methods of execution violate the Eighth Amendment protection against cruel and unusual punishment.

A particularly strong argument against capital punishment centers around the inconsistency with which the penalty is imposed. In other words, why are only select individuals who could receive capital punishment sentenced to death? Foster (2001, p. 17) lists variables found *within the criminal justice system* that help explain why "we get from 20,000 homicides to 300 death-sentenced inmates each year." The variables include:

1. Whether the state in which the offense was committed has a death penalty law.
2. The breadth of the state's death penalty statute. For instance, the statute may or may not incorporate murders of law enforcement officers, or contract killings.
3. The prosecutor's attitude toward capital punishment.
4. The competency of defense counsel and the quality and quantity of supporting resources at her or his disposal.
5. The attitude of the victim's family. For instance, prosecutors may not pursue a death penalty verdict if the victim's family is opposed.
6. The attitudes and willingness of the jury to impose a death penalty (Foster, 2001, pp. 17, 19).

In addition to identifying the variables found with the legal system, Foster identifies a different series of variables that also help explain the inconsistency of the death penalty. These variables *directly relate to the crime and criminal,* including:

1. The race and class of the victim. Offenders who victimize middle-class and white victims are more likely to receive the death penalty.

2. The innocence of the victim. For instance, defendants face a greater likelihood of being executed when they kill a 4-year-old as opposed to when they kill a violent drug dealer.

3. The number of victims. Murdering a greater number of victims increases the likelihood of execution.

4. The heinousness of the crime. For instance, did the offense involve torture?

5. The offender's criminal history. Prior felony and murder convictions increase the likelihood of the death penalty.

6. Clarity of the evidence. Strong evidence increases the likelihood of capital punishment.

7. Remorse, or the lack of. Those showing no remorse for their actions are more likely to face the death penalty.

8. Residency status. Transients seem to be at a disadvantage in capital trials, particularly when they kill an individual with local ties (Foster, 2001, pp. 19–20).

Recent research by Bonczar and Snell (2004) sheds light on capital punishment in the United States. For instance, they note that 65 inmates were executed by 11 states and the Federal government in 2003, six fewer than were executed in 2002. All 65 inmates executed were male; 41 were white, 20 were black, three were Hispanic, and one was American Indian. All but one of the executions were by lethal injection (the other was by electrocution). The 65 executions in 2003 was the lowest total number of executions since 1996 when there were 45. Texas (24, or 36.9%) executed the greatest number of inmates in 2003, although California had the greatest number of prisoners under a sentence of death (624, or 18.6% of the 3,374 prisoners under a sentence of death). Most of those under a sentence of death were white (54%) (Bonczar & Snell, 2004). Only 47 females were under a sentence of death in 2003, however, this number is notably higher than the 38 females sentenced to death in 1993 (Bonczar & Snell, 2004).

Recent evidence suggests a change may be underway with regard to public support and the use of capital punishment. For instance, the Supreme Court, which until recently assumed a hands-off approach to capital punishment, offered several major decisions regarding the death penalty. For instance, the 2002 decision in *Atkins v. Virginia* prohibits the execution of mentally retarded offenders, whereas in *Ring v. Arizona* (2002) the Court overruled part of an earlier decision and determined that capital defendants are entitled to have juries impose (or recommend to a judge) a death sentence following examination of aggravating circumstances (Foster, 2006). Trial judges in Arizona formerly made such decisions without input from a jury. In 2004, the Court prohibited the imposition of the death penalty on offenders who were under the age of 18 when their crimes were committed (*Roper v. Simmons*).

Bonczar and Snell (2004) note that the 3,374 inmates under a sentence of death at yearend 2003 was 188 fewer inmates than at yearend 2002. They attribute the decrease, in large part, to the removal of 267 inmates from a sentence of death in 2003. They add that "Illinois accounted for 60% of these removals: the governor (George Ryan) removed all inmates from under sentence of death when he commuted 155 death sentences and granted 4 pardons" (Bonczar & Snell, 2004, p. 8).

WRAP-UP

Our examination of incarceration helps us better understand what James can expect in prison and how he relates to the prison population. Like many others in prison, James has a criminal record. Whether he actually makes good use of his time in prison, for instance, through taking advantage of betterment programs, or whether he will merely serve his time and return to society no better than when he entered remains to be seen. Should James choose to "correct" his problems, he may find difficulty securing the treatment and counseling he needs as the current philosophical approach to corrections stresses incapacitation, deterrence, and retribution.

Most of us have strong opinions regarding incarceration and/or the death penalty. As such, American corrections remains very controversial. In a country as large and diverse as America there are going to be differences of opinion on criminal justice policy. Human emotions become charged and the debate intensifies when the policy involves taking one's life or severely restricting freedoms. It is unlikely that we will soon find the perfect solution to addressing crime and criminals, yet such pessimism should not stop our quest for answers.

Point–Counterpoint

HIV/AIDS in prison affects correctional officers and inmates on a daily basis. A controversial approach to addressing the issue is to test and segregate those who are HIV-positive or have AIDS. While prisons earlier separated infected inmates from the general prison population, fears surrounding the spread of the disease have subsided, resulting in a dramatic decline in the number of facilities segregating those testing positive for HIV or AIDS (Braithwaite, Hammett, & Mayberry, 1996). *Should prisons test and segregate those testing positive for HIV/AIDS?*

Yes: The overall rate of AIDS in prison is three times the rate in the general public. Mass testing inmates and segregating those testing positive for HIV/AIDS makes sense. Prisoners are more likely than the general public to engage in acts associated with the transfer of the disease (e.g., use dirty needles, have a history of multiple sex partners, etc.), thus testing and segregating will protect inmates, corrections personnel, and the general public, given that 99% of offenders return to society. Segregating prisoners who test positive for HIV/AIDS allows prison officials to identify those with the diseases and closely monitor their behavior, particularly with regard to risky behaviors. The segregated group becomes a target group for educational and counseling sessions (e.g., pre-vention counseling regarding the spread of the disease). Segregating these individuals provides correctional officers greater protection in the sense that they are cognizant of which inmates have the disease.

No: There are several reasons why prisons moved away from segregating HIV/AIDS-infected inmates. To begin, segregation results in labeled or stigmatized inmates, which could lead to them being treated or viewed as less worthy than those in the general population. Furthermore, segregated inmates are often denied rights and opportunities available to other inmates, including having limited, if any, access to religious exercises, recreational activities, and opportunities for prison employment. In order to segregate those testing positive we must first test each inmate, which generates numerous problems, not the least of which is the questionable accuracy of the tests and the associated costs of testing. There are also logistical problems associated with segregation, including the need for duplicity of services. Efforts to provide equal services will be required. Perhaps the strongest argument against segregation concerns findings that the risk of transmitting the diseases through casual contact is extremely low. The belief that the disease could be transmitted through casual contact is inaccurate, as it is now understood that a much higher degree of interaction between individuals is required for the spread of the disease.

SUGGESTED READING

Kerle, K. E. (1998). *American jails: Looking to the future.* Boston: Butterworth-Heinemann.

McShane, M. D., & Williams, F. (Eds.). (1996). *Encyclopedia of American prisons.* New York: Garland.

Nelson, L., & Foster, B. (2001). *Death watch: A death penalty anthology.* Upper Saddle River, NJ: Prentice Hall.

Ross, J. I., & Richards, S. C. (2002). *Behind bars: Surviving prison.* Indianapolis, IN: Alpha.

Welch, M. (1994). Jail overcrowding: Social sanitation and the warehousing of the underclass. In A. Roberts (Ed.), *Critical issues in crime and justice* (pp. 249–274). Thousand Oaks, CA: Sage.

CRITICAL THINKING EXERCISES

1. Aside from the legal and crime/criminal variables discussed above as affecting the likelihood of a murder resulting in a death penalty case, what other variables do you believe would affect whether or not a case will have life or death implications?

2. Compare the demographic profile of jail inmates, prisoners, and those sentenced to death. Explain the similarities and differences.

3. How could we make the death penalty more consistent? Consider and discuss ways in which imposition of capital punishment could be more consistent across jurisdictions.

SHORT ESSAY QUESTIONS

1. Discuss why jails are vital in the U.S. system of justice. What functions do they serve?

2. Compare and contrast the three models of incarceration that have been prominent in corrections since the 1940s.

3. Discuss the various levels of prisons. Do you feel it is fair for most white-collar offenders to be sentenced to minimum-security prisons? Why or why not?

4. Discuss who is in jail and explain why they are there.

5. Summarize the costs of incarceration and identify ways in which you believe the costs could be reduced.

14 RELEASE AND REENTRY

James served 37 months of his 6-year prison sentence. He was eligible for parole after 2 years; however, a parole board in his first petition for release denied James parole based on the seriousness of the offense for which he was incarcerated, his criminal history, and his lack of participation in "betterment" programs. They suggested James take advantage of the prison's job skills and anger management programs. One year later James was granted parole and released with a bus ticket and $50. He immediately contacted and eventually moved in with a cousin who arranged a job for James. Upon release from prison, James, unlike many other former inmates, avoided criminal behavior. He maintained steady employment and successfully completed the terms of his parole. James was released from the criminal justice system following 3 years of supervision in the community.

Inmates are released from prison in several ways, although discretionary release and mandatory release are used in a large majority of cases. These two forms of release are conditional in the sense that inmates will be released early; however, they will be subject to community supervision by a parole authority. Inmates are also released from prison following the expiration of their sentence. Inmates who "max out" are released to the community without any conditions or supervision, regardless of whether or not they are rehabilitated or prepared for reentry. Those serving the entirety of their sentence typically spent only a short period incarcerated in jail or prison (Clear & Dammer, 2000).

Various factors make release from prison difficult for many offenders. Aside from the difficulties of being labeled an "ex-con," losing particular privileges such as the right to vote (10 states permanently remove offenders' right to vote following one felony conviction), the right to hold public office, and/or the right to enter into contracts, some former inmates struggle to adjust to life outside prison without the state providing for them. Difficulties such as the need to reestablish ties with family members, secure employment, and survive financially hamper many offenders. Furthermore, many inmates leave prison without addressing the issues that contributed to their incarceration. For instance, some inmates are released to society and still have substance abuse problems, limited job skills, and/or mental illnesses. Thomas (2002, p. 9) notes: "Most states have drastically cut funding for education, drug rehab, and job training in prisons and have abolished early release for good behavior: all programs that could have helped prisoners readjust to the outside world."

PAROLE

Similar to probation, parole involves a period of conditional supervision in the community. Parole differs from probation primarily in the sense that parole always occurs following a period of incarceration. Parolees must abide by particular conditions set forth in a parole contract until the maximum expiration date (i.e., the date on which their sentence expires) if they wish to be released from correctional supervision. Champion (1999) identified the reintegration of parolees into society and the control and/or deterrence of crime as the two primary functions of parole. He adds that parole serves the latent functions of easing prison and jail overcrowding, remedying sentencing disparities, and protecting the public.

Two primary forms of parole exist: discretionary parole and mandatory parole. Discretionary parole, which is associated with the rehabilitation model and indeterminate sentencing, involves parole board members using their discretionary authority to release or continue detaining an inmate following a statutory or administratively defined period of time. Mandatory release is generally used in states with determinate sentencing structures, which became increasingly popular in the 1980s. It involves the early, conditional release of inmates whose sentence was reduced as a result of earned good time. Clear and Dammer (2000, p. 190) note that mandatory release is akin to "bookkeeping to ensure that the correct amount of good-time and other credits have been allocated and that the court's sentence has been accurately interpreted so that the offender moves automatically into the community at the expiration of the period." Good-time credit is viewed as encouragement or an incentive for inmates to participate in self-help programs and comply with prison rules. Prison officials often use the threat of losing good time to control inmate behavior.

Parole is currently undergoing significant changes. While most inmates on parole traditionally were sanctioned in jurisdictions using indeterminate sentencing practices and faced discretionary release following a period of incarceration, mandatory release is currently used to determine the release date of most inmates. Particularly, 50% of inmates faced a parole board in 1995, while 45% received mandatory parole. These percentages changed following the elimination of discretionary parole in several states. For instance, only 37% of inmates were released at the discretion of a parole board in 2000, while 54% received mandatory parole.

Hughes, Wilson, and Beck (2001) note that 69% of those released from state prison in 1977 went before a parole board, when 44 states and Washington, D.C., used discretionary release. They add that eight states eliminated discretionary parole during the 1990s and "Most of the remaining States further restricted parole by setting specific standards offenders must meet to be eligible for release" (p. 2). At year-end 2000, 16 states and the federal government had abolished parole boards as a means of releasing offenders. Another four states had removed the power of parole boards to release particular violent offenders.

Furthermore, those presently being released are subject to parole officers emphasizing *surveillance* as opposed to *assistance*, although both components are vital to parole. Seiter and Kadela (2003, p. 361) note that inmates in general are serving longer prison stints, with "only a small percentage. . .receiving the benefit of extensive rehabilitation or pre-release programs. The communities are more disorganized, their families are less likely to be supportive, and the releasees find fewer social services available to them in the community."

THE USE AND ADMINISTRATION OF PAROLE

The U.S. adult parole population, which stood at 774,588 at year-end 2003, increased 3.1% between 2002–2003, a notably higher percentage than the 1.7% average annual increase since 1995. The 3.1% increase was the largest single year increase between 1995 and 2003 (Glaze & Palla, 2004), and attributable to the increased use of incarceration. For instance, Hughes and colleagues (2001, p. 2) note that the percentage of state inmates receiving parole grew at a slower rate than the state prison population between 1990 and 2000. They note that on average, the prison population annually increased by 5.7%, while the parole population annually increased by 2.6%. They suggest that "The low rate of growth in parole supervision reflects changes in sentencing and parole release policies that have resulted in increasing lengths of stay in prison and declining prison release rates." The recent 3.1% increase of the parole population could be a sign that the increased use of incarceration will soon have an even greater impact on parole.

There were 357 adults on parole for every 100,000 U.S. residents at yearend 2003. Seventeen states had double-digit increases in the percentage of their parole populations between 2002–2003, led by a 53% increase in North Dakota. Females constituted 13% of those on parole in 2003, a 3% increase from 1995. Roughly the same percentage of parolees were black (41%) as were white (40%), and 95% of parolees were convicted of a felony (Glaze & Palla, 2004).

The United States Parole Commission is the paroling authority at the federal level, with field services administered by the Administrative Office of the Courts. Each state is responsible for administering parole within its boundaries, and each state has its own paroling authority, which falls under the jurisdiction of the executive office.

Three organizational models are used to administer parole services. The *institutional model* uses members from within the inmate's institution to determine parole eligibility. Familiarity with the inmate is a primary benefit of this model, however, factors unrelated to the offender's suitability for release (e.g., institutional factors such as overcrowding) may influence the decisions of institutional members. The institutional model is more ingrained in the juvenile justice system than in adult corrections (McCarthy et al., 2001).

Parole decisions are made by individuals outside the inmate's institution in the *autonomous model.* Supporters of the autonomous model argue that those outside of the inmate's institution can make a more objective assessment than those within the institution regarding the inmate's suitability for parole. A concern with the autonomous model is the lack of familiarity between parole board members and inmates (McCarthy et al., 2001).

The *consolidated model* of parole attempts to address the limitations of the autonomous and institutional models by having individuals from within and outside the inmate's institution assess suitability for parole. McCarthy and colleagues (2001) note that institutional members in the consolidated model do not maintain the authority to release inmates; however, they offer input to parole officials from outside of the institution who also sit on the board. The consolidated model seems to be the preferred model of parole administration in adult corrections.

PAROLE PERSONNEL

Parole board members, who in most states are politically appointed and serve terms of 6 years or less (McCarthy et al., 2001), serve two primary functions: assessing inmate suitability for parole and policy development. Being a parole board member is, in some places, a full-time job with a competitive salary. In other areas, board members volunteer their time to serve and in return receive a small honorarium and expenses (Clear & Dammer, 2000). Either way, placement on a parole board requires expertise in criminal justice and human behavior.

Parole board members are often assisted by a preparole investigation report, similar to the PSI prepared for sentencing judges. The report, prepared by institutional staff (often parole officers assigned to the prison), contains vital information on the inmate and is used to evaluate their suitability for parole (Clear & Dammer, 2000).

Understanding the views of parole board members helps us understand the use of discretionary parole. A survey of parole board members found that the lack of support for parole by the public was the most serious problem facing parole boards, and better treatment-based programs within prison would be the best way to improve the parole process. Furthermore, it was found that parole board members justify parole based on the rehabilitative and reintegrative benefits, and they consider the nature and circumstances of the inmate's offense and the inmate's prior record as the two most important release criteria (Burns, Kinkade, Leone, & Phillips, 1999). Clear and Dammer (2000) note that failure to provide an acceptable parole release plan, which describes what the inmate will do upon release (e.g., employment, housing, treatment), is the most common reason for the denial of parole.

Parole officers provide supervisory services for parolees and clearly shape modern parole practices. They serve many of the same functions as probation officers; in fact, the parole board administers the combined parole and probation services in most states (McCarthy et al., 2001). Parole officers perform both law enforcement and social services. Law enforcement services include ensuring parolees comply with the terms of their parole agreement and monitoring their behavior in the community. Referring parolees to treatment centers and assisting with job searches are among the social service contributions of parole officers.

BEING RELEASED ON PAROLE

The rate at which inmates are granted parole varies by state, although states that permit inmates to have a parole hearing early in their sentence generally have lower rates of release than do states that require inmates to serve a longer period of incarceration prior to going before a parole board (Clear & Dammer, 2000).

Some jurisdictions using discretionary release permit parole boards to determine the minimum parole eligibility date. In other jurisdictions the minimum date is set by the courts or a statute. Should the inmate not be released following the first appearance, the parole board may set dates for a future hearing and assess the inmate's progress. The dates for a parole hearing are often prescribed by statute (e.g., parole hearings may occur on an annual basis), although parole boards sometimes establish a parole contract with individuals in an attempt to encourage them to meet specific requirements within a specified timeframe. Inmates will be released upon meeting the requirements.

In granting inmates parole, board members establish conditions to which the inmate must agree and subsequently abide by upon release. The conditions typically serve the purposes of helping offenders live crime-free lives and assisting parole officers with their supervisory duties. Parole board members also hear cases involving parole revocation in addition to cases of inmates up for parole. The parole hearing occurs in a meeting room (not in a courtroom) and the typical hearing is very short in duration, often lasting only a few minutes.

Most states have incorporated due process rights into the parole release hearing. Clear and Dammer (2000, p. 192) note that "about half the states now allow counsel to be present and witnesses to be called and keep verbatim transcripts." They add that most parole authorities now immediately provide the parolee written or verbal explanation of the decision, adding that such changes are "a far cry from the earlier practices, when the inmate went alone into a 'roomful of strangers,' spent maybe five minutes before the board, and later was informed in writing only that parole had been 'granted' or 'denied'" (p. 192).

There is controversy surrounding who should be involved in the parole hearing and what should be discussed (e.g., Clear & Dammer, 2000). For instance, some jurisdictions prohibit inmates from appearing, and some permit testimony of family members and friends. Recent practices include victims in the parole hearing. Clear and Dammer (2000) note that most jurisdictions provide for victim input via personal appearance or victim advocates.

SUCCESS AND FAILURE ON PAROLE

Joan Petersilia (2003) describes life for those exiting prison under conditions of parole:

> Most [parolees] will be given a bus ticket and told to report to the parole officers in their home community on the next business day. . . . If they live in a state that provides funds upon release (about one-third of states do not), they will be given $25 to $200 in gate money. Some states provide a new set of clothing at release, but these extras. . .have declined over time. Sometimes, a list of rental apartments or shelters is provided, but the arrangements are

generally left up to the offender to determine where to reside and how to pay for basic essentials such as food, housing, and clothing during the first months. (p. 7)

The transition from prison to society can be troubling for many offenders for several reasons, including the difficulties associated with being released from prison yet remaining under supervision. One of the greatest struggles for released inmates involves securing and maintaining employment. Uncomfortable site visits from a parole officer, the hesitancy of employers to hire parolees, and the stigma attached with being an "ex-con" provide hurdles for parolees seeking employment. A lack of literacy and overall job readiness provide additional obstacles for many parolees. Released inmates in many jurisdictions also face civil restrictions such as losing the right to vote or hold public office, although some states restore inmate rights following completion of their sentence. The strangeness of reentry and the problem of unmet personal needs (e.g., job, money, housing) are among other barriers to success that contribute to the discouragingly high percentage of parolees who return to prison.

There are two types of parole revocation. The first results from the commission of a new offense while under parole supervision. Revocation could also result from a technical violation or an act that is not criminal; however, it violates the terms of the parole agreement. The commission of a new offense or a technical violation does not necessarily result in parole revocation. In fact, overcrowded prisons have reduced the likelihood of parole violators returning to prison. Some parole officers use their discretion to overlook some technical violations. The more serious action of committing a new offense typically results in parole revocation hearings.

The parole revocation process begins with a parole board assessing whether or not there is reasonable cause to believe a legal or technical violation occurred. Should the case move forward, the second step is a hearing to determine whether or not the offender will return to prison. Parolees retain particular due process rights at revocation hearings (e.g., *Morrissey v. Brewer,* 1972) involving technical violations, including the right to confront witnesses; written notice of the charges against them; present testimony and witnesses and/or evidence on their behalf; and a written statement justifying the reasoning behind the final decision.

Recent research by Glaze and Palla (2004) found that just under half (47%) of the 470,500 parolees discharged from supervision in 2003 successfully met the terms of their conditions. This success rate is slightly higher than the rates of previous years such as 1995 (45% success rate) and 2000 (43% success rate). A substantial portion (38%) of the remaining parolees discharged from supervision in 2003 were incarcerated as a result of a new offense or a rule violation. Aside from incarceration, alternative sanctions for parole violations include the loss of parole time (i.e., the offender must spend a greater amount of time on parole) and an enhanced level of supervision (e.g., more stringent conditions and/or more frequent visits from a parole officer).

OTHER FORMS OF RELEASE

In addition to the three aforementioned types of release (discretionary release, mandatory release, and maxing out), there are other forms of release from prison. These alternative methods of release are used infrequently compared to discretionary and mandatory release.

Clemency "is a policy that states that executive or legislative action can reduce the severity of the punishment, waive the legal punishment of one or more individuals, or even exempt individuals from prosecution for certain actions" (Clear & Dammer, 2000, pp. 193–194). Clemency is used, for instance, in cases where evidence emerges post-conviction exonerating a prisoner. The four forms of clemency are pardons, amnesty, commutation, and reprieve. *Pardons* involve a government official restoring the rights and privileges of convicted individuals, for instance to correct a miscarriage of justice. Former U.S. President Richard Nixon was pardoned for any involvement in the Watergate scandal by his successor, former U.S. President Gerald Ford. *Amnesty* is similar to a pardon, although it applies to a group or class of offenders (e.g., when the U.S. grants amnesty to illegal aliens). *Commutations* involve the shortening or changing of prison sentences, for instance, when inmates become terminally ill, or when death sentences are reduced to sentences of life in prison. *Reprieves* are temporary postponement of the execution of a sentence, and are most often associated with capital punishment. They are considered temporary release and typically do not result in offenders being permanently released from incarceration (Clear & Dammer, 2000).

TEMPORARY RELEASE

As noted, release from prison is challenging for many inmates as they transition from prison life to life in society. Some jurisdictions offer temporary release programs through which inmates can slowly readjust to society. The goal in many states is to gradually reintroduce the inmate to society. Temporary release programs help combat the effects of "prisonization" or institutionalization by granting inmates short periods of time in society, following which they return to prison. For instance, *work release* provides inmates an opportunity to reorient themselves with life and work outside the prison walls, while sometimes serving the secondary goal of providing the offender with particular job skills. *Study release*, a similar program, provides offenders time outside prison to attend classes and further their education or learn job skills. Inmates are expected to return to prison each day following their student-related obligations. Inmates are sometimes granted *furloughs*, which enable them to leave prison for extended periods of time (typically 24 to 72 hours) for various reasons, such as reestablishing family ties or searching for housing in anticipation of an upcoming release.

McCarthy and colleagues (2001) note that among other things, temporary releases facilitate offender reintegration; help manage and control inmate behavior through the threat of removing such privileges; demonstrate a humanitarian side of the criminal justice system in showing concern for the inmate; and provide another area of evaluation in determining one's potential suitability for return to society. On the other hand, temporary releases provide another avenue through which inmates can violate regulations (e.g., returning late or intoxicated from release). Absconding and criminal behavior while on temporary release are also concerns associated with temporary release.

WRAP-UP

Continued prison construction reduces the amount of resources available to help inmates, for instance, with regard to their reentry to society. Given increasing incarceration rates and overcrowding concerns, states are building new prisons at the expense of programs for current inmates. In response, those returning to society may be less prepared and unable to successfully adjust. While eliminating prison programs may seem cost-effective, the relatively high rate of parolees returning to prison is, in the long run, more expensive. Petersilia (2003, p. 3) notes that "About three-quarters of all prisoners have a history of substance abuse, and one in six suffers from mental illness. Despite these needs, fewer than one-third of exiting prisoners receive substance abuse or mental health treatment while in prison."

So what can be done? Petersilia (2003, p. vi) notes the existence of programs both in and out of prison that can help inmates live within the boundaries of the criminal law. She states, "Community-based organizations, local businesses, and faith-based organizations are showing themselves to be critical partners in assisting offenders with their transitions. Some states have made important beginnings, and their programs are reducing recidivism and saving money." James Austin (2001, p. 314) argues that "For most inmates, reentry should be curtailed by either eliminating supervision or greatly shortening the period of supervision." He offers this suggestion in response to the significant portion of parolees returned to prison for technical violations or misdemeanor offenses.

Point–Counterpoint

Shifts toward "truth in sentencing laws" and the increasing percentage of inmates maxing out leave some wondering about the future of parole. Parole remains prominent in society despite this recent trend. In light of these and related issues, *should we abolish parole?*

Yes: Parole results in increased danger to society. Offenders should serve the sentence they receive, and apparently deserve. In other words, parole distorts justice as inmates don't serve the penalties associated with their behavior. Furthermore, we must question whether or not parole truly meets the goal of rehabilitation; many would claim that parole has little rehabilitative effect. The discretion granted to parole board members can result in harmfully incorrect decisions that hurt innocent victims and the image of the criminal justice system. Finally, the relatively high rate of return to prison by parolees suggests that we do not use parole properly, as we are letting a notably large percentage of inmates free to continue their criminal ways.

No: Parole is helpful to offenders, the criminal justice system, and society in general. Among other things, parole provides a cost savings as the state no longer is required to provide for all aspects of an inmate's well-being. Parole acts as an agent of social control in prisons by encouraging inmates to behave or they'll lose their opportunity for early release. Parole can also be used to correct injustices. For instance, offenders, on occasion, will receive extraordinarily harsh sentences following emotional cases and/or sentencing hearings. In turn, parole can serve to correct the injustice. Parole increases the likelihood of restitution and rehabilitation, both of which are unlikely while offenders remain incarcerated. The argument that parolees are a danger to society is tempered by research that suggests that most released inmates pose very little, if any, threat to society. Finally, parole is necessary given current concerns regarding prison overcrowding. Parole is not the problem. The manner in which it is being used, however, with emphasis on surveillance and reduced concern for assistance, limits a parolee's chances for success.

SUGGESTED READING

Austin, J., & Hardyman, P. L. (2004). The risk and needs of the returning prisoner population. *Review of Policy Research, 21*(1), 13–29.

Hughes, T. A., Wilson, D. J., & Beck, A. J. (2001, October). *Trends in state parole, 1990–2000* (NCJ 184735). Washington, DC: National Institute of Justice, Bureau of Justice Statistics.

McShane, M. D., Williams, F. P. III, & Dolny, H. M. (2003). The effect of gang membership on parole outcome. *Journal of Gang Research, 10*(4), 25–38.

Petersilia, J. (2003). *When prisoners come home: Parole and prisoner reentry.* New York: Oxford University Press.

Seiter, R. P., & Kadela, K. R. (2003). Prisoner reentry: What works, what does not, and what is promising. *Crime & Delinquency, 49*(3), 360–388.

CRITICAL THINKING EXERCISES

1. How are the majority of prisoners released in your home state? Visit the Web site for the state agency responsible for parole in your state and comment on the nature of prisoner release (e.g., How many are released annually? By what means are they released?)

2. Given recent trends in prisoner release, forecast what will become of parole 20 years from now. Will parole be abolished or refined? More or less popular? Will it be discretionary?

3. Assume you are the public relations director for the state Department of Corrections. A recent parolee was accused of brutally murdering an elderly woman. The media is asking how this could happen. What steps would you take to address the situation?

SHORT ESSAY QUESTIONS

1. Discuss the recent changes in parole and the effects these changes will have on parolees.

2. Discuss the parole revocation process. How does this compare to probation revocation?

3. Identify and discuss the differences between the various types of temporary release from prison.

4. Much has been written about parole board members. What roles are served by parole board members and what factors do they consider in determining whether or not to release an inmate from prison?

5. Identify and discuss the difficulties faced by inmates as they readjust to society. What steps can be taken to address the difficulties?

EPILOGUE

We've now journeyed through the criminal justice system. To be sure, actual criminal case processing is very different, and far more complex than what is portrayed in the media and seen on television and in movies. This book covers the "nuts and bolts" of criminal case processing, while foregoing in-depth discussion of any particular component of criminal justice. Readers interested in going deeper into any of the areas discussed in this work are strongly encouraged to peruse the extensive volumes of work that detail the intricacies and nuances of policing, the courts, and corrections. Some of the more informative pieces are identified within and at the end of each chapter.

When we think of *criminal justice*, we often focus on law enforcement, courts, and corrections. However, we must not neglect the integral role we all play in the daily functioning of our justice systems. No account of the criminal justice system would be complete without recognizing the contributions society makes to the criminal justice system. For instance, individual participation in criminal case processing involves, among other things, reporting crime, testifying as witnesses, serving on juries, employing probationers and parolees, and electing politicians who support (or don't support) criminal justice legislation. Public fear of crime and citizen responses to particular crimes also provide direction for criminal justice policy and reactions. Consider, for instance, the manner in which student individual rights and freedoms have been restricted in response to a series of high-profile school shootings.

The fictitious case study involving James demonstrates one approach to criminal case processing. It was designed to help readers follow one man's trip through the system. James's case was, in some ways, atypical of what happens to those in James's position (e.g., he went to trial), yet representative of criminal case processing in many other ways (e.g., he couldn't afford representation). James's case could have gone in multiple directions, as criminal case processing is influenced by numerous variables.

Unfortunately, the criminal justice system is filled with too many cases such as James's, resulting in a slew of unanswered questions. For instance, what do we do given the large number of cases such as James's? Should we continue to rely on the criminal justice system to address crime? And by "address" do we mean prevent and/or respond to crime? Where and how should we prevent crime (e.g., in schools, in the streets, in corporate offices, via public service announcements, providing greater public assistance)? How should we respond to crime (e.g., prisons, more police, greater community involvement, tougher sentences)?

The answers to these and many other, related questions may never be answered. We can be sure, however, that the criminal justice system faces many challenges in the years ahead. I am not a futurist and cannot, with a strong level of confidence, forecast what will happen in the future. With consideration of historical trends and a particular focus on the past century, however, I can speculate as to what I see impacting the criminal justice system. To begin, numerous social events significantly impacted the criminal justice system, and there's every reason to believe that future significant events will have additional impacts. For instance, prohibition in the early 20th century and the civil rights movement of the 1960s and 1970s had incredibly large effects on policing. Prohibition was a time when organized crime groups gained a strong footing and police corruption attracted significant societal interest. Similarly, the ongoing war on drugs has altered the criminal justice system in ways few could have imagined.

The 2001 terrorist attacks on the United States changed law enforcement in many ways. One effect has been the change in public support for police officers. For instance, there was an outpouring of support for police officers following the deaths of many New York City officers who lost their lives in the attacks while trying to save others. Furthermore, police officers now have an enhanced duty to protect against, and recognize, terrorist threats. Following the attacks, President George W. Bush outlined areas of improvement with regard to homeland security. In particular, he noted the need to protect against biological and chemical attacks; improve intelligence gathering and law enforcement coordination; provide greater control at airports and borders; and enhance emergency response (de Guzman, 2002). To be sure, these tasks are not solely placed on federal law enforcement agencies. What was once seen by many as the job of federal law enforcement, protecting against terrorism has become well situated in local law enforcement. The terrorist attacks brought a significant change to the organization of federal law enforcement. Most notably, the Department of Homeland Security was created following the attacks with the intent to provide a more cohesive approach to federal law enforcement. De Guzman (2002, p. 9) suggests that the attacks of September 11, 2001, "are by themselves sufficient motivation or provocation for police departments to re-examine themselves and adjust their tactics to the demands of the time."

Technology has undoubtedly influenced the criminal justice system. From onboard computers in police patrol cars to centralized databases containing information accessible from anywhere in the world, technology is changing the manner in which criminal justice agencies operate. Technology is finding its way into courts and corrections, for instance, by permitting judges to electronically access case law during court proceedings and the use of technology in facilitating offender supervision (e.g., electronic monitoring). While technology has certainly enhanced our fight against crime, it also poses a new and daunting challenge for criminal justice agencies. For instance, local law enforcement agencies believe they are ill-prepared to confront Internet fraud (Burns, Whitworth, & Thompson, 2004), one of the fastest growing technology-based crimes.

Sherman (2002, p. 22) notes that "Criminal justice is far less corrupt, brutal, and racially unfair than it has been in the past. It is arguably more effective at preventing crime. It has far greater diversity in its staff." He adds, however, that recent Gallup polls show public confidence in the criminal justice system is low relative to other institutions such as television news, newspapers, big business, and organized labor. Based on recent progress, we can expect continued professional development of criminal justice agencies in the years ahead. Increased training requirements and more selective recruitment practices are but two reasons for increased professional development in law enforcement and corrections. Greater judicial accountability has undoubtedly contributed to increasingly professional courtroom proceedings. We've come to expect greater professionalism from public officials as we continue to rely on the criminal justice system to address crime. We've made significant progress in this area, although there certainly remains room to grow. Given recent developments, one can expect criminal justice agencies to become more accountable and subsequently more professional. Let's hope public confidence in the justice system keeps pace with the development.

An increasingly shrinking globe certainly affects the American system of justice. Greater international commerce, communication, and travel have impacted society and provided avenues for new and lucrative criminal opportunities. Our decentralized system of justice discourages interstate cooperation with regard to crime and justice; however, the problems associated with limited interstate cooperation seem minimal when one considers the lack of international cooperative crime-fighting efforts. The changing nature of crime brings with it the need for U.S. justice agencies to look beyond our borders, as we can no longer turn a blind eye to transnational crime. It will be interesting to observe the responses by justice agencies in all countries as society further develops and crime continuously adopts an international flavor.

White-collar crime will continue to impact the criminal justice system. White-collar crimes were historically ignored by many justice agencies, however, recent events hint toward, and highlight a need for, a change in practice. Martha Stewart and executives at Tyco, Enron, and Adelphia were involved in just a few of the high-profile white collar crimes recently brought to societal attention. In addition to the high-profile cases, we must keep in mind the many white-collar crimes we don't hear about. The recent series of white-collar crime cases encouraged the federal government to pass the *Sarbanes–Oxley Act of 2002,* which grants the President power to select a Corporate Fraud Task Force designed to offer recommendations on efforts to enforce financial crime laws. The act also includes severe penalties for altering or destroying vital documents, restrictions on personal loans from companies to top administrators, and new regulations to address the conflict of interest among financial analysts and corporations. Furthermore, the act extends the time period for victimized investors to file civil charges for fraudulent activity. Historically, the criminal justice system has assumed a seemingly disinterested approach to investigating and enforcing white-collar crime. Recent efforts suggest we can expect criminal justice agencies to take a more active effort in recognizing and enforcing white-collar crimes.

Consider the criminal justice system of half a century ago, when there was less professionalism and accountability in all three components of the system. Now consider how far we've come in the fight against crime and the search for justice. Imagine how officers in the 1950s would have reacted if you told them that in 50 years patrol cars will have computers onboard. Think of how judges would have reacted if you told them that technology such as videotaped testimony and the electronic presentation of evidence would become part of their courtroom. Imagine the reaction of Ward Cleaver if you told him that instead of going to prison, some offenders would be monitored at their home with the assistance of an electronic bracelet that would contact authorities should the offender leave the confines of their home. Who knows what criminal justice will be like 50 years from now? Let's hope we don't need criminal justice; however, let's be realistic . . . crime likely isn't going to disappear.

Our best efforts to reach the utopian goal of a crime-free society begins with an understanding of crime and justice, and the factors influencing each. Developing the knowledge necessary to reach our goal is certainly easier said than done. However, each successful marathon runner begins their journey with a first step. We're beyond a first step in our understanding of crime and justice; however, we certainly have a long way to go—the marathon is far from complete. This work sheds light on the day-to-day functioning of criminal justice agencies and personnel. Knowledge and sound application of that knowledge will help us attain our goals. Hopefully, by reading this book you've gained a more complete understanding of how the system works and can use your knowledge to help ensure that ours is truly a system of criminal *justice.*

REFERENCES

Adler, F., Mueller, G. O. W., & Laufer, W. S. (2003). *Criminal justice: An introduction* (4th ed.). Boston: McGraw-Hill.

Anderson, R. A. (1957). *Wharton's criminal law and procedure* § 1724. Rochester, NY: Lawyers Co-operative Publishing.

Austin, J. (2001). Prisoner reentry: Current trends, practices, and issues. *Crime & Delinquency, 47*(3), 314–334.

Barkan, S. E., & Bryjak, G. J. (2004). *Fundamentals of criminal justice.* Boston: Allyn & Bacon.

Bayley, D. (1994). *Police for the future.* New York: Oxford University Press.

Bennett, R. R., & Wiegand, R. B. (1994). Observations on crime reporting in a developing nation. *Criminology, 32*(1), 135–148.

Bennett, W., & Hess, K. (2001). *Criminal investigation* (6th ed.). Belmont, CA: Wadsworth.

Blaauw, E., Vermunt, R., & Kerkhof, A. (1997). Detention circumstances in police stations: Towards setting the standards. *Policing and Society, 7,* 45–69.

Black, D. (1980). *Manners and customs of the police.* San Diego, CA: Academic Press.

Black, D. (1983). Crime as social control. *American Sociological Review, 48,* 34–45.

Block, R. (1974). Why notify the police: The victim's decision to notify the police of an assault. *Criminology, 11,* 555–569.

Bohm, R. M., & Haley, K. N. (2002). *Introduction to criminal justice* (3rd ed.). New York: McGraw-Hill.

Bonczar, T. P. (2003, August). *Prevalence of imprisonment in the U.S. population, 1974–2001* (NCJ 197976). Washington, DC: U.S. Department of Justice, Bureau of Justice Statistics.

Bonczar, T. P., & Snell, T. L. (2004, November). *Capital punishment, 2003* (NCJ 206627). Washington, DC: U.S. Department of Justice, Bureau of Justice Statistics.

Borum, R., & Fulero, S. M. (1999). Empirical research on the insanity defense and attempted reforms: Evidence toward informed policy. *Law and Human Behavior, 23*(1), 117–135.

Braithwaite, R., Hammett, T., & Mayberry, R. (1996). *Prisons and AIDS: A public health challenge.* San Francisco: Josey-Bass.

Brandl, S. (1993). The impact of case characteristics on detectives' decision making. *Justice Quarterly, 10*(3), 395–416.

Briggs, C. S., Sundt, J. L., & Castellano, T. C. (2003). The effect of supermaximum security prisons on aggregate levels of institutional violence. *Criminology, 41,* 1341–1376.

Brooks, L. W. (2005). Police discretionary behavior: A study of style. In R. G. Dunham & G. P. Alpert (Eds.), *Critical issues in policing: Contemporary readings* (5th ed.; pp. 89–105). Prospect Heights, IL: Waveland.

Burns, R. (2002). Assessing jail coverage in introductory criminal justice textbooks. *Journal of Criminal Justice Education, 13*(1), 87–100.

Burns, R., & Crawford, C. (2002). Situational determinants of police violence. In R. Burns & C. Crawford (Eds.), *Policing and violence* (pp. 73–100). Upper Saddle River, NJ: Prentice Hall.

Burns, R., Kinkade, P., Leone, M. C., & Phillips, S. (1999). Perspectives on the parole process: The board members' viewpoint. *Federal Probation, 63*(1), 16–22.

Burns, R. G. (1996, July/August). Boot camps: The empirical record. *American Jails,* pp. 42–49.

Burns, R. G., Whitworth, K. H., & Thompson, C. Y. (2004). Assessing law enforcement preparedness to address Internet fraud. *Journal of Criminal Justice, 32*(5), 477–493.

Chaiken, J., Greenwood, P., & Petersilia, J. (1977). The criminal investigation process: A summary report. *Policy Analysis, 3,* 187–217.

Chambliss, W. J. (Ed.). (1984). *Criminal law in action.* New York: McGraw-Hill.

Champion, D. J. (1998). *Criminal justice in the United States* (2nd ed.). Chicago: Nelson-Hall.

Champion, D. J. (1999). *Probation, parole, and community corrections* (3rd ed.). Upper Saddle River, NJ: Prentice Hall.

Clear, T. R., & Cole, G. F. (2003). *American corrections* (6th ed.). Belmont, CA: Wadsworth.

Clear, T. R., & Dammer, H. R. (2000). *The offender in the community.* Belmont, CA: Wadsworth.

Cohen, R. L. (1995, August). *Probation and parole violators in state prison, 1991* (NCJ 149076). Washington, DC: Bureau of Justice Statistics.

Cole, G. F. (1970). The decision to prosecute. *Law and Society Review, 4*(3), 331–343.

Cole, G. F., & Smith, C. E. (2004). *The American system of criminal justice* (10th ed.). Belmont, CA: Wadsworth.

Conaway, M. R., & Lohr, S. L. (1994). A longitudinal analysis of factors associated with reporting violent crimes to the police. *Journal of Quantitative Criminology, 10*(1), 23–39.

Daly, K. (1987). Discrimination in the criminal courts: Family, gender, and the problem of equal treatment. *Social Forces, 66*(1), 152–175.

Dattu, F. (1998, September/October). Illustrated jury instructions. *Judicature, 82*(2), 79.

DeFrances, C. J., & Litras, M. F. X. (2000, November). *Indigent defense services in large counties, 1999* (NCJ 184932). Washington, DC: U.S. Department of Justice, Bureau of Justice Statistics.

De Guzman, M. (2002). The changing roles and strategies of the police in time of terror. *ACJS Today, XXII*(3), 8–13.

del Carmen, R. (2004). *Criminal procedure: Law and practice* (6th ed.). Belmont, CA: Wadsworth.

Durose, M. R., & Langan, P. A. (2004, December). *Felony sentences in state courts, 2002* (NCJ 206916). Washington, DC: U.S. Department of Justice, Bureau of Justice Statistics.

Dutton, P. M. (1999, July). *Mental health and treatment of inmates and probationers* (NCJ 174463). Washington, DC: U.S. Department of Justice, Bureau of Justice Statistics.

Eck, J. (1984). *Solving crimes.* Washington, DC: Police Executive Research Forum.

Elias, R. (1986). *The politics of victimization: Victims, victimology and human rights.* New York: Oxford University Press.

Eskridge, C. W. (1999). Justice and the American justice network. In C. W. Eskridge (Ed.), *Criminal justice: Concepts and issues* (3rd ed., pp. 11–18). Los Angeles: Roxbury.

Fagin, J. A. (2003). *Criminal justice.* Boston: Allyn & Bacon.

Federal Bureau of Investigation. (2003). *Crime in the United States 2002.* Washington, DC: U.S. Department of Justice.

Feeley, M. (1979). *The process is the punishment: Handling cases in a lower criminal court.* New York: Russell Sage.

Ferdico, J. N. (1996). *Criminal procedure for the criminal justice professional* (6th ed.). St. Paul, MN: West.

Foglia, W. D. (2003). They know not what they do: Unguided and misguided discretion in Pennsylvania capital cases. *Justice Quarterly, 20*(1), 187–211.

Foster, B. (2001). How the death penalty really works: Selecting death penalty offenders in America. In L. Nelson & B. Foster (Eds.), *Death watch: A death penalty anthology* (pp. 16–21). Upper Saddle River, NJ: Prentice Hall.

Foster, B. (2006). *Corrections: The fundamentals.* Upper Saddle River, NJ: Prentice Hall.

Franklin, R. H. (1998). Assessing supermax operations. *Corrections Today, 60*(4), 126–127.

Gaines, L., Kappeler, V., & Vaughn, J. (1999). *Policing in America* (3rd ed.). Cincinnati, OH: Anderson.

Gaines, L. K., & Miller, R. L. (2003). *Criminal justice in action* (2nd ed.). Belmont, CA: Wadsworth.

Gilboy, J. A. (1984, Winter). Prosecutors' discretionary use of the grand jury to initiate or to reinitiate prosecution. *American Bar Foundation Research Journal, 9*(1), 1–81.

Glaser, D. F. (1995). *Preparing convicts for law-abiding lives: The pioneering penology of Richard A. McGee.* Albany: State University of New York Press.

Glaze, L. E., & Palla, S. (2004, July). *Probation and parole in the United States, 2003* (NCJ 205336). Washington, DC: U.S. Department of Justice, Bureau of Justice Statistics.

Goldfarb, R. (1975). *Jails: The ultimate ghetto.* Garden City, NY: Doubleday.

Goldkamp, J. (1979). *Two classes of accused: A study of bail and detention in America.* Cambridge, MA: Ballinger.

Goldstein, H. (1977). *Policing a free society.* Cambridge, MA: Ballinger.

Gottfredson, M. R., & Gottfredson, D. M. (1988). *Decision making in criminal justice: Toward the rational exercise of discretion* (2nd ed.). New York: Plenum Press.

Gottfredson, M. R., & Hindelang, M. J. (1979). A study of the behavior of law. *American Sociological Review, 44,* 3–18.

Greenwood, P. W., Chaiken, J. M., & Petersilia, J. (1977). *The criminal investigation process.* Lexington, MA: Heath.

Hanson, R. A., & Daley, H. W. K. (1995, September). *Federal habeas corpus review: Challenging state court criminal convictions* (NCJ 155504). Washington, DC: U.S. Department of Justice, Bureau of Justice Statistics.

Hanson, R. A., & Ostrom, B. J. (2002). Indigent defenders get the job done and done well. In G. F. Cole, M. G. Gertz, & A. Bunger (Eds.), *The criminal justice system: Politics and policies* (8th ed.; pp. 254–277). Belmont, CA: Wadsworth.

Harlow, C. W. (1985). *Reporting crimes to the police: Bureau of Justice Statistics Special Report.* Washington, DC: U.S. Government Printing Office.

Harlow, C. W. (2000, November). *Defense counsel in criminal cases* (NCJ 179023). Washington, DC: U.S. Department of Justice, Bureau of Justice Statistics.

Harrison, P. M., & Beck, A. J. (2004, November). *Prisoners in 2003* (NCJ 205335). Washington, DC: U.S. Department of Justice, Bureau of Justice Statistics.

Harrison, P. M., & Karberg, J. C. (2004, May). *Prison and jail inmates at midyear 2003* (NCJ 203947). Washington, DC: U.S. Department of Justice, Bureau of Justice Statistics.

Hart, T. C., & Rennison, C. (2003, March). *Reporting crime to the police, 1992–2000* (NCJ 195710). Washington, DC: U.S. Department of Justice, Bureau of Justice Statistics.

Hess, K. M., & Wrobleski, H. M. (2003). *Police operations: Theory and practice* (3rd ed.). Belmont, CA: Wadsworth.

Hickman, M. J., & Reeves, B. A. (2003). *Local police departments 2000* (NCJ 196002). Washington, DC: U.S. Department of Justice, Bureau of Justice Statistics.

Hindelang, M. J., & Gottfredson, M. (1976). The victim's decision not to invoke criminal justice process. In W. F. McDonald (Ed.), *Criminal justice and the victim* (pp. 57–78). Beverly Hills, CA: Sage.

Hughes, T. A., Wilson, D. J., & Beck, A. J. (2001, October). *Trends in state parole, 1990–2000* (NCJ 184735). Washington, DC: National Institute of Justice, Bureau of Justice Statistics.

Irwin, J. (1985). *The jail: Managing the underclass in American society.* Berkeley: University of California Press.

Jackson, P. G. (1987). The impact of pretrial preventive detention. *Justice System Journal, 12*(3), 305–334.

James, D. J. (2004, July). *Profile of jail inmates, 2002* (NCJ 201932). Washington, DC: U.S. Department of Justice, Bureau of Justice Statistics.

Kappeler, V., & Potter, G. (2005). *The mythology of crime and criminal justice* (4th ed.). Long Grove, IL: Waveland.

Katz, C. M., & Spohn, C. C. (1995). The effect of race and gender on bail outcomes: A test of an interactive model. *American Journal of Criminal Justice, 19*(2), 161–184.

Kidd, R. F., & Chayet, E. F. (1984). Why do victims fail to report? The psychology of criminal victimization. *Journal of Social Issues, 40*(1), 39–50.

Klinger, D. A. (1996). More on demeanor and arrest in Dade County. *Criminology, 34,* 61–82.

Kloberdanz, K. (2005, March 21). Building a better lineup. *Time,* p. 19.

Kuykendall, J. (1986). The municipal detective: An historical analysis. *Criminology, 24*(1), 175–201.

Langan, P., Greenfeld, L., Smith, S., Durose, M., & Levin, D. (2001). *Contacts between police and the public: Findings from the 1999 national survey* (NCJ 184957). Washington, DC: U.S. Department of Justice, Bureau of Justice Statistics.

Lyman, M. D. (1999). *The police: An introduction.* Upper Saddle River, NJ: Prentice Hall.

Lynch, M. J., Michalowski, R., & Groves, W. B. (2000). *The new primer in radical criminology: Critical perspectives on crime, power & identity* (3rd ed.). Monsey, NY: Criminal Justice Press.

Mahoney, B., Beaudin, B. D., Carver, J. A. III, Ryan, D. B., & Hoffman, R. B. (2001, March). *Pretrial services programs: Responsibilities and potential* (NCJ 181939). Washington, DC: U.S. Department of Justice, National Institute of Justice.

Maruschak, L. M. (2004, January). *HIV in prisons, 2001* (NCJ 202293). Washington, DC: U.S. Department of Justice, Bureau of Justice Statistics.

Mastrofski, S. D., Worden, R. E., & Snipes, J. B. (1995). Law enforcement in a time of community policing. *Criminology, 33,* 539–563.

McBride, D., & VanderWaal, C. (1997). Day reporting centers as an alternative for drug using offenders. *Journal of Drug Issues, 27*(2), 379–398.

McCarthy, B. R., McCarthy, B. J. Jr., & Leone, M. C. (2001). *Community-based corrections* (4th ed.). Belmont, CA: Wadsworth.

McGinley, H., & Pasewark, R. A. (1989). National survey of the frequency and success of the insanity plea and alternative pleas. *Journal of Psychiatry and Law, 17,* 205–221.

Morgan, K. D. (1993, June). Factors influencing probation outcome: A review of the literature. *Federal Probation,* pp. 23–29.

Morton, J. B. (2001). Implications for corrections of an aging prison population. *Corrections Management Quarterly, 5*(1), 78–88.

National Advisory Commission on Criminal Justice Standards and Goals. (1973). *Report on courts.* Washington, DC: U.S. Government Printing Office.

Neubauer, D. W. (1991). Winners and losers: Dispositions of criminal appeals before the Louisiana Supreme Court. *Justice Quarterly, 8*(1), 85–105.

Neubauer, D. W. (1999). *America's courts and the criminal justice system* (6th ed.). Belmont, CA: Wadsworth.

Neubauer, D. W. (2005). *America's courts and the criminal justice system* (8th ed.). Belmont, CA: Wadsworth.

Pagelow, M. D. (1984). *Family violence.* New York: Praeger.

Palmer, C. A., & Hazelrigg, M. (2000). The guilty but mentally ill verdict: A review and conceptual analysis of intent and impact. *Journal of the American Academy of Psychiatry and the Law, 28,* 47–54.

Perkins, C. A., Stephan, J. J., & Beck, A. J. (1995, April). *Jails and jail inmates 1993–1994: Census of jails and survey of jails* (NCJ 151651). Washington, DC: U.S. Department of Justice, Bureau of Justice Statistics.

Petersen, R. D., & Palumbo, D. (1997). The social construction of intermediate punishments. *The Prison Journal, 77*(1), 77–91.

Petersilia, J. (1997, September). Probation in the United States: Practices and challenges. *National Institute of Justice Journal, 233,* 2–8.

Petersilia, J. (2003). *When prisoners come home: Parole and prisoner reentry.* New York: Oxford University Press.

Petersilia, J., & Deschenes, E. P. (1994). Perceptions of punishment: Inmates and staff rank the severity of prison versus intermediate sanctions. *The Prison Journal, 74*(3), 306–328.

Petersilia, J., Turner, S., Kahan, J., & Peterson, J. (1985). *Granting felons probation: Public risks and alternatives.* Santa Monica, CA: Rand Corporation.

President's Commission on Law Enforcement and Administration of Justice. (1967). *Task force report: Science and technology.* Washington, DC: Government Printing Office.

Pyszczynski, T. A., & Wrightsman, L. S. (1981). The effects of opening statements on mock jurors' verdicts in simulated trials. *Journal of Applied Social Psychology, 11*(4), 301–313.

Quindlen, A. (2002, January 21). Lights, camera, justice for all. *Newsweek, 139,* 64.

Rackmill, S. J. (1994, March). An analysis of home confinement as a sanction. *Federal Probation,* pp. 45–52.

Rainville, G., & Reaves, B. A. (2003, December). *Felony defendants in large urban counties, 2000* (NCJ 202021). Washington, DC: U.S. Department of Justice, Bureau of Justice Statistics.

Reaves, B. A., & Hickman, M. (2002). *Police departments in large cities, 1990–2000* (NCJ 175703). Washington, DC: U.S. Department of Justice, Bureau of Justice Statistics.

Reiss, A. J. Jr. (1971). *The police and the public.* New Haven, CT: Yale University Press.

Report to the Attorney General on Delays in Forensic DNA Analysis (NCJ 199425). (2003). Washington, DC: National Institute of Justice, U.S. Department of Justice.

Riksheim, E. C., & Chermak, S. M. (1993). Causes of police behavior revisited. *Journal of Criminal Justice, 21,* 353–382.

Rosen, L. (1995). The creation of the Uniform Crime Report. *Social Science History, 19*(2), 215–238.

Ross, J. I., & Richards, S. C. (2002). *Behind bars: Surviving prison.* Indianapolis, IN: Alpha.

Ruback, B. R., Greenberg, M. S., & Westcott, D. R. (1984). Social influence and crime-victim decision making. *Journal of Social Issues, 40,* 51–76.

Rush, G. E. (2003). *The dictionary of criminal justice* (6th ed.). Guilford, CT: Dushkin/McGraw-Hill.

Scheb, J. M., & Scheb, J. M. II. (2003). *Criminal procedure* (3rd ed.). Belmont, CA: Wadsworth.

Schmalleger, F. (2005). *Criminal justice today* (8th ed.). Upper Saddle River, NJ: Prentice Hall.

Seiter, R. P., & Kadela, K. R. (2003). Prisoner reentry: What works, what does not, and what is promising. *Crime & Delinquency, 49*(3), 360–388.

Senna, J. J., & Siegel, L. J. (2002). *Introduction to criminal justice* (9th ed.). Belmont, CA: Wadsworth.

Shapland, J., Willmore, J., & Duff, P. (1985). *Victims in the criminal justice system.* Brookfield, VT: Gower.

Shelden, R. G., & Brown, W. (2003). *Criminal justice in America: A critical view.* Boston: Allyn & Bacon.

Sherman, L. (1980). Causes of police behavior: The current state of quantitative research. *Journal of Research in Crime and Delinquency, 17,* 69–100.

Sherman, L. W. (2002). Trust and confidence in criminal justice. *National Institute of Justice Journal, 248,* 22–31.

Skogan, W. (1976). Citizen reporting of crime: Some national panel data. *Criminology, 13*(4), 535–549.

Skogan, W. (1977). Dimensions on the dark figure of unreported crime. *Crime & Delinquency, 23,* 41–50.

Smith, D. A., & Klein, J. R. (1984). Police control of interpersonal disputes. *Social Problems, 31,* 468–481.

Smith, D. A., & Visher, C. A. (1981). Street-level justice: Situational determinants of police arrest decisions. *Social Problems, 29*(2), 169–177.

Sparks, R. F., Genn, H. G., & Dodd, D. J. (1977). *Surveying victims: A study of the measurement of criminal victimization, perceptions of crime, and attitudes to criminal justice.* Chichester, UK: Wiley.

Spelman, W. (1995). The severity of intermediate sanctions. *Journal of Research in Crime and Delinquency, 32*(2), 107–135.

Spelman, W. G., & Brown, D. K. (1984). *Calling the police: Citizen reporting of serious crime.* Washington, DC: Police Executive Research Forum.

Steadman, G. W. (2002). *Survey of DNA crime laboratories, 2001* (NCJ 191191). Washington, DC: Bureau of Justice Statistics, U.S. Department of Justice.

Steele, W. W. Jr., & Thornburg, E. G. (1991). Jury instructions: A persistent failure to communicate. *Judicature, 74*(5), 249–254.

Stephan, J. J. (2004, June). *State prison expenditures, 2001* (NCJ 202949). Washington, DC: U.S. Department of Justice, Bureau of Justice Statistics.

Stephan, J. J., & Karberg, J. C. (2003, August). *Census of state and federal correctional facilities, 2000* (NCJ 198272). Washington, DC: U.S. Department of Justice, Bureau of Justice Statistics.

Stuckey, G. B., Roberson, C., & Wallace, H. (2004). *Procedures in the justice system* (7th ed.). Upper Saddle River, NJ: Prentice Hall.

Supreme Court Finds No Violation in Ban on Polygraph Evidence. (1998, March 3). *Criminal Justice Newsletter,* pp. 3–4.

Survey of State Criminal History Information Systems (NCJ 200343). (2003). Washington, DC: U.S. Department of Justice, Bureau of Justice Statistics.

System Improves Sheriff's Department's Tracking. (1997, Fall). *American City & County, 112,* p. 32.

Territo, L., Halsted, J. B., & Bromley, M. L. (2004). *Crime and justice in America: A human perspective.* Upper Saddle River, NJ: Prentice Hall.

Thomas, S. (2002, October). War on whom? *Friends Journal,* pp. 8, 9, 44.

Thompson, J. (1986). The American jail: Problems, politics, and prospects. *American Journal of Criminal Justice, 10,* 205–221.

Tonry, M. (1988). Intermediate sanctions. In M. Tonry (Ed.), *The handbook of crime and punishment* (pp. 683–711). New York: Oxford University Press.

U.S. Probation and Pretrial Services. (2003, January). *Court and community: An information series about U.S Probation and Pretrial Services.* Washington, DC: Office of Probation and Pretrial Services, Administrative Office of the U.S. Courts.

Visher, C. (1987). Incapacitation and crime control: Does a "lock 'em up" strategy reduce crime? *Justice Quarterly, 4,* 513–544.

Waegel, W. (1981). Case routinazation in investigative police work. *Social Problems, 28*(3), 263–275.

Walker, S. (2001). *Sense and nonsense about crime and drugs* (5th ed.). Belmont, CA: Wadsworth.

Walker, S., & Katz, C. (2002). *Police in America: An introduction* (4th ed.). Boston: McGraw-Hill

Welch, M. (1994). Jail overcrowding: Social sanitation and the warehousing of the underclass. In A. Roberts (Ed.), *Critical issues in crime and justice* (pp. 249–274). Thousand Oaks, CA: Sage.

Wernicke, S. C., & Stallo, M. A. (2000, July). Steps toward integrating crime analysis into local law enforcement. *The Police Chief,* pp. 56–57.

Weston, P. B., & Lushbaugh, C. (2003). *Criminal investigation: Basic perspectives* (9th ed.). Upper Saddle River, NJ: Prentice Hall.

William, M., & Snortum, J. (1984). Detective work: The criminal investigation process in a medium-size police department. *Criminal Justice Review, 9,* 33–39.

Williams, F. P. III. (1981). The impact of discretion on station-house release. *American Journal of Police, 1*(1), 1–22.

Williams, J. J. (1991). Predicting decisions rendered in criminal appeals. *Journal of Criminal Justice, 19,* 463–469.

Willing, R. (2005, March 17). Courts try to make jury duty less of a chore. *USA Today,* pp. 17A–18A.

Worrall, J. L., & Hemmens, C. (2005). *Criminal evidence: An introduction.* Los Angeles: Roxbury.

Wrobleski, H., & Hess, K. (2003). *Introduction to law enforcement and criminal justice* (7th ed.). Belmont, CA: Wadsworth.

Argersinger v. Hamlin, 407 U.S. 25 (1972). 32

Atkins v. Virginia, 536 U.S. 304 (2002). 93

Douglas v. California, 372 U.S. 353 (1963). 68

Fay v. Noia, 372 U.S. 391 (1963). 70

Furman v. Georgia, 408 U.S. 238 (1972). 91

Gagnon v. Scarpelli, 411 U.S. 778 (1973). 78

Gregg v. Georgia, 428 U.S. 153 (1976). 91–92

Hurtado v. California, 110 U.S. 516 (1884). 40

McNabb v. U.S., 318 U.S. 332 (1943). 32

Mempa v. Rhey, 389 U.S. 128 (1967). 78

Morrissey v. Brewer, 408 U.S. 471 (1972). 100

Ring v. Arizona, 536 U.S. 584 (2002). 93

Roper v. Simmons, 112 SW 3d 397, affirmed. 93

Ross v. Moffitt, 417 U.S. 600 (1974). 68

INDEX

118   INDEX